Forged In Struggle: From Brokenness to Redemption

Aaron Belleri
Forged In Struggle: From Brokenness to Redemption

—

Published by - Spines
ISBN: 979-8-89691-304-7

Forged In Struggle: From Brokenness to Redemption

Book 1: The Descendants of Lemech

Aaron Belleri

BROKENESS

Always remember 🌸

"When life breaks you, it is because you are ready to be put back together differently.

Every piece of you that feels shattered is a piece that will find a new place, a new purpose, a new meaning.

Trust that the cracks are where the light gets in. And sometimes, in our brokenness, we find our greatest wholeness.

We find the courage to rebuild, to reimagine, to redefine what it means to be strong.

You are not broken; you are breaking through."

---Unknown

I want to thank God for giving me the courage and inspiration to share this story of faith, resilience, hope and love. No matter what we go through in life we must ask Him to grant us discernment, so that we may see the lesson He is trying to teach us; and the wisdom and knowledge to understand it.
---By the Author

Forged In Struggle:
From Brokenness to Redemption

A dimly lit, run-down city street, reflecting the struggles he's faced. The atmosphere is heavy, filled with the sounds of the city—honking horns, distant sirens, and the murmurs of people passing by.

"Indulging in sin is pleasurable at first, but in the end, it is empty and bitter. I know this better than most." My name is David Argum and this is my story...

Whispers of Temptation

David, limping slightly, navigates the streets, his face a mix of determination and weariness. Despite the pain in his joints, there's a fire in his eyes that suggests he's not completely defeated. He clutches a worn-out backpack, its contents a mix of necessities and remnants of a life he's trying to leave behind.

As he walks, David reflects on his past—brief flashes of memories: the chaos of his childhood home, the loneliness of abandonment, the cold nights spent homeless, the stinging regret of his prison years. Each memory is a ghost that haunts him, reminding him of the choices he made and the pain he carries.

He passes a group of people enjoying themselves at a bar, laughter spilling out into the street. For a moment, he hesitates, caught between the allure of that world and the bitter reality of his own life.

He shakes off the thoughts, continuing on his path, but not without a lingering sense of longing. "I thought I could escape it all," he muses. "But every high has its low, and I'm still chasing something I can't quite define."

THE BURDEN OF CHOICES

David shifted the weight of his backpack, the strap digging into his shoulder, a dull reminder of all he had left. As he passed the bar, he caught his own reflection in the window—a face hardened, eyes that looked older than his years, and a limp that made each step a reminder of the disease gnawing at his joints. Once, this place might have pulled him in; a drink to drown the weight of everything he carried, a random encounter with some young woman or some cocaine to round the night out, but tonight, he kept walking.

It had only been a few days since he'd gotten out of jail, empty-handed. Four days earlier, he'd been pulled over, cuffed, and thrown behind bars for a list of infractions that felt both petty and punishing: no license, no insurance, a suspicion of other crimes that hadn't yet surfaced. But even that didn't sting as much as what he'd lost when they towed his car—a faded but loyal '98 Mercedes. His sole possession, his only way of moving beyond the radius his body could handle.

Scattered Pieces

Inside that car had been his life, reduced to belongings that, piece by piece, told the story of his survival. The clothes on his back, his tools, his souvenirs,

anything that grounded him—lost, like sand slipping through his fingers. The rest of his things left in the hotel room he and Sandi shared...gone, stolen by thieves.

The final blow came when he learned what Sandi had done. While he sat in jail, counting hours with a creeping dread, she'd left. She didn't wait, didn't even pretend to care. She moved on in the flash of an opportunity, packing her things and moving in with a new man, choosing the security of someone else's bed over the uncertainty of David's.

He pushed back the bitterness that rose up in his chest. Sandi's true colors were only a reminder of what he'd come to expect, of the cycles that had chained him for years.

As David walked through the darkened streets, a new kind of weariness settled over him. Over the past year, he had come through for more people than he could count. Friends—old and new—who had reached out when they needed help, and he'd been there. A ride across town, cash when they were short, a place to crash for the night. Food, drugs, whatever they needed to get by. He hadn't thought twice about it back then; it was the kind of loyalty he'd been raised on, twisted by hardship but unbreakable—or so he'd believed.

But now, as he scrolled through his phone, staring at one dead-end after another, he realized just how alone he was. He called everyone he could think of, anyone who might be willing to help him with just one night off the streets, but excuses and quick rejections were all he received. The same voices that once welcomed his generosity now turned him away, too busy or too broke to offer anything back.

He'd spent the last two nights sleeping outside, wherever he could find a patch of ground that felt safe enough. The ache in his bones had grown sharper on the hard ground, his body protesting each rough night. The streets had a way of stripping a man bare, exposing him to the kind of truths he'd never faced when he was the one holding the keys, the cash, the comfort.

Tonight, though, he felt that clarity seeping in, the nights were relentless—hot, humid, and thick with the smell of the bay and garbage left to bake in the day's sun.

Each time he tried to settle, the humid air clung to his skin, and the relentless bite of mosquitoes left him restless, swatting in vain as they feasted on his exposed arms and neck. Every inch of him ached from lying on unforgiving ground, his body protesting as if the heat itself had found a way to sink into his bones. The hot wind blowing a fine mix of dirt and sand stuck to his sweaty body.

There was no escape, no relief in sight. On the third day, just as David felt his resolve beginning to waver, a glimmer of hope surfaced in an unexpected place.

Panda—a friend who was barely scraping by himself, bouncing from one seedy motel to the next—picked up the phone.

VOICES IN THE WILDERNESS

"Man, I don't have much," Panda admitted, his voice rough and weary, but genuine. "But if you need a shower, come through. Got A/C, too." We heard about your troubles; there's someone here who wants to see you too.

It was more kindness than David had been shown in days, and the thought of a cool shower and a moment of respite felt like a blessing. The motel was run-down, the kind of place that looked even sadder in daylight, but it was shelter. As David stepped into the room, the wave of cool air wrapped around him, and the sight of a familiar face—even one worn down by the same struggles—gave him a quiet sense of relief.

David had just settled in, letting the cool air slowly revive him, when the door creaked open. He looked up, surprised, as a familiar figure stepped through. It was Crystal. He hadn't seen her in years, but here she was, as if no time had passed. Crystal's expression brightened when she saw him.

"David!" she said, shaking her head in disbelief. "Why didn't you call me?"

He gave her a small, tired smile. "I didn't even think about it, Crystal. You usually have enough on your plate. Didn't want to burden you with my mess."

Crystal scoffed and came over, reaching out as if to ground him with a steady hand on his shoulder. "If I got it, you got it. We look out for each other."

A familiar warmth settled between them, an understanding built over years of shared struggle. It was an unspoken pact, a bond they'd both held onto despite the ups and downs of their lives.

As David sat there, letting the silence settle over him, the weight of everything began to press down, deeper and sharper than the physical discomfort of the past few days. His car, his dog, the few possessions that had felt like anchors—gone, like dust swept away in a storm. And then there was Sandi, slipping from his life just as easily as she'd entered it, taking something intangible but essential with her. He was so happy to be off the streets and among friends, but at the same time, David wanted to cry for all he had lost.

He tried to shake her from his mind, but she lingered there, a shadow he couldn't escape. It was like she had imprinted herself somewhere deep, refusing to be pushed away. Every time he tried to think of a next move, a plan to claw his way back up, his mind circled back to her. Why was she still in his head? Why, when she'd already moved on so easily, did he feel so tethered to her, as if he were under a spell cast by her memory?

David spent those days in a daze, relying on Crystal to keep the room, the food, and a steady supply of meth—the only thing that seemed to dull the edges of his reality. She covered it all without complaint, a quiet ally when he had nothing left. But he knew it couldn't last, and that thought weighed on him, mingling with a creeping guilt. He could see the weariness in her, but she never spoke of it, and he never asked.

Through the haze, his thoughts always found their way back to Sandi. He could still remember the early days, that feeling of ease and assurance she brought him.

She had known just what to say, just how to make him feel whole, respected even, in ways he hadn't felt in years. The memories of them camping, roughing it together at the state park or on that quiet dead-end road, Skinner Ln., came back to him as vivid and bittersweet as an old melody. Back then, he hadn't thought twice about leaving his sister's place, abandoning stability for her, because Sandi had made everything seem right. She'd made him feel like a king, like there was no place he'd rather be than by her side, no matter how bare the circumstances.

But it all came apart, slowly, imperceptibly at first. That feeling she had given him—the one he clung to like a lifeline—began to slip away. And the more it slipped, the more he tried to hold onto it, like sand slipping through his fingers. He kept trying to fix things, to put the broken pieces back together, forgiving more than he ever thought he would, all in the hope of recapturing that feeling. It felt like a habit he couldn't shake, an endless chase for something lost but unforgettable, just like that first high he once knew.

Two weeks passed in a blur. Each day, David found himself torn between reaching out for help and just surrendering to the fog of his life as it was. Crystal, though stretched thin herself, continued supporting him in every way she could, but the weight of dependence began to press on Crystal. Something inside him — a distant voice that had stayed silent for so long—began to whisper that he needed to make a change.

The Idea of leaving Texas came up more often in his thoughts, growing clearer each time. And then there was Eddy's voice in his mind, almost like a chant: "Come to Colorado. Start fresh. Let me help." It felt like a beckoning.

David hadn't seen or even thought about Eddy in years until Eddy had reached out. The timing was uncanny, almost as if Eddy had known, somehow, just how low David would sink.

One evening, after Crystal had left to run some errands, and Panda had gone the night before and never returned, David found himself alone in the quiet motel room. He glanced around at his few belongings, feeling the overwhelming weight of his circumstances pressing in. The phone lay on the nightstand, and before he had time to reconsider, he dialed Eddy's number.

A Friend in Need

"David!" Eddy's voice came through, as warm and welcoming as it had been all those years ago in that Houston, TX. jail cell. "Man, I've been waiting to hear from you. You ready to come up here yet?"

David hesitated, swallowing hard. "I don't even know how I'd get there, Eddy. I'm not in great shape. I lost my car, and—"

"Forget the details," Eddy interrupted, his tone firm. "You get to Denver, and I'll handle the rest. You need this, David. You know you do. This isn't just some spur-of-the-moment thing. It's time."

David felt something inside him stir. It was that old restlessness, but now it felt different—a kind of yearning he couldn't shake off. It wasn't just escape he was after; there was something else, something deeper calling to him. And though he didn't fully understand it, he decided he was done trying to figure it out from where he was.

"All right," he said, his voice barely above a whisper. "I'll come."

Eddy's laughter, full of relief and encouragement, echoed through the receiver. "Good. That's good, man. You're making the right choice. Let's get you here, and we'll take it from there."

That night, David lay awake, feeling both apprehension and a strange sense of hope. For so long, he'd held onto Sandi, the life he'd tried to build, the constant chase to keep everything patched together.

But now, for the first time in a long time, he felt like he was moving toward something unknown, and for once, he didn't feel afraid.

As the first light of dawn crept over the horizon David made his way out of the motel, each step feeling lighter than the last. Colorado awaited, and though he didn't know what he'd find there, he felt a certainty that whatever it was, it would be different from anything he'd known, but he had a few loose ends to tie up here in Texas first.

The next day David sat on the edge of the bed, the room dim in the early morning haze, with Crystal still asleep on the couch. His mind was heavy, churning with all that had happened. In two short weeks, his thoughts had returned to Sandi and then drifted, as they always did, back to the helpless question: Where did it all go wrong?

But now, something unexpected crept in, a small nudge beneath the weight of regret and anger—a reminder of a voice from a distant past. Eddy.

They had barely known each other back in that Houston lock-up, just two guys with rough pasts waiting to see what the system had in store for them. But somehow, they'd connected in that bleak space. Eddy's stories of life up in the mountains, of finding clarity and peace, had stayed with David. He hadn't realized it until now, but Eddy's words had planted a seed, the idea of some place untouched by the pain of the past. And over the past year, Eddy's messages had come through every now and then, always the same encouragement: Come up here, man. Start fresh. There's something different here.

David pulled out his old phone, the cracked screen lighting up as he scrolled through his messages, searching for Eddy's last one.

It's still open, David, it read. Come to Denver. Nothing's stopping you but you.

David let out a long sigh. Maybe there was nothing left to lose.

SHADOWS OF THE PAST

Lost in thought, overwhelmed by recent events. As he watches the sun set, he remembers another sunset—a time when he and Jamie, the girl he was with prior to Sandi, sat on the hood of his car, talking late into the night. They were discussing their dreams and fears, and through the memory, he realizes how deeply Jamie affected him, why he carries such unresolved feelings, and what he's searching for that which he lost with her. Jamie had been the one person to teach David something about himself that he'd been blind to—His selfishness.

That night, as he finally sank into the lumpy motel mattress, the room's dim hum gave way to an unusual quiet, the kind of quiet that pulls you under, deep and fast. The night was heavy with his plans for the morning: the bus ticket in his email Eddy had sent him, a decision that was half hope and half desperation. Still, in sleep, his mind wandered somewhere else entirely.

DREAMS

He was standing on a wide, open field under a deep, golden sunset, the sky streaked with pink and orange—just like that evening with Jamie, years before. He looked down and there she was, her silhouette leaning against the hood of his old car, her blonde hair blowing across her face. She turned to look at him, that familiar spark in her eyes, like she was seeing right through every wall he'd built up.

"You remember this night?" she asked softly, a faint smile playing on her lips. Her voice was warm, bringing with it the bittersweet rush of memories he'd thought he'd buried long ago.

David nodded, words catching in his throat. He remembered everything—how they'd parked out in the middle of nowhere, far from anyone else, feeling like they were the only two people in the world. He remembered the way she laughed as they talked about the future, and the way she'd gripped his hand as if she never planned to let go.

In the dream, he wanted to reach out, to pull her closer and ask her why she'd left. But his feet felt rooted to the ground, heavy with regret.

"You always kept one foot out the door, David." Jamie whispered, her voice turning soft, almost sad. "You were always planning your escape, even when I was right here." She looked down, as if remembering a part of him he'd hidden from himself.

"But I tried," he murmured, feeling an ache rise in his chest. "I did everything I knew how to do."

Her eyes met his, filled with both love and a deep, quiet disappointment. "Maybe that's the problem, David, you never knew how to let yourself be loved. You were always waiting for the hurt, expecting it. And maybe that's why it found you."

Before he could answer, a sharp wind blew across the field, and she was gone. He called her name, his voice hollow against the empty sky, but there was nothing. Only silence.

David woke with a start, his heart pounding, the weight of her words still lingering, sharp as a fresh wound. The room was dark, the same stale scent hanging in the air, but the ache in his chest felt as real as if she'd been right there beside him.

He lay back, staring at the ceiling, letting the memory of Jamie settle around him like a ghost he couldn't shake. As he closed his eyes, he felt the familiar ache, the pull toward something he had chased all his life but never truly found.

As David drifted back into a restless sleep, the ocean came alive in his dreams. He found himself standing barefoot on a stretch of sand, waves rushing over his feet in cool, rhythmic patterns, and the scent of salt hung thick in the air. In the distance, Jamie appeared, walking toward him. Her blond hair caught the last light of sunset, each strand glowing softly in the amber glow.

She came closer, her eyes warm yet tinged with an unspoken sadness, a gaze that held all the moments they'd once shared. Jamie didn't say a word, yet her presence stirred something deep within him—a mix of memories, regrets, and a tenderness he'd tried to bury. She reached out, her fingers gently brushing his face as if to comfort him, and for a moment, he could feel everything he'd lost. He had loved Jamie with all his heart.

They stood together in silence, the waves crashing softly around them, an David felt that familiar ache, the haunting reminder of how things had unraveled. The ocean seemed to stretch endlessly, a symbol of the distance between where they'd been and where he was now.

As they stood by the shore, David felt an urge to speak, to say something that would somehow bridge the chasm time and choices had placed between them. But when he tried to speak, the words seemed trapped, caught somewhere between his heart and his throat. Jamie just looked at him, her hand resting softly on his cheek, as if she understood everything, he couldn't bring himself to say.

Then she leaned in, close enough that he could feel the warmth of her breath against his skin, and whispered, "It's not too late." Her voice was soft but firm, like the tide itself, carrying an unshakable certainty. She smiled, a bittersweet smile that seemed to hold both forgiveness and farewell. With that, she took a step back, her hand slipping away from his face, and turned toward the water.

David reached for her, but his feet seemed heavy, rooted in the sand. He watched as Jamie walked deeper into the ocean; her silhouette illuminated by the fading glow of the sun. She was calm, serene, almost like a ghost merging with the waves, until she disappeared beneath the surface, leaving only ripples on the water that quickly faded into the vast, undisturbed expanse of the sea.

He woke with a jolt, the final image of Jamie's retreating form lingering vividly in his mind. The ache was still there, but her words echoed within him, their simple truth reverberating in his chest. "It's not too late."

Job 33:29—"Behold, God does all these things, twice, three times, with a man, to bring his soul back from the pit, that he may be lighted with the light of life."

Thoughts

Sitting on the edge of the bed, David took a deep, weighted breath, looking out at the flickering motel sign outside the window. Shadows shifted across the room, and he caught himself in a loop of memories, each one another tumble downwards—a pit deeper than the last. How many times had he thought he'd found solid ground, only to have it fall away again?

He closed his eyes and muttered, "Twice, three times, God does this... to bring a man back from the pit... to light his soul." The words from Job settled on him, a verse buried in his mind from those days his great aunt Beatrice would read to him, her voice like a slow, steady balm.

What if there was a purpose to this endless digging up of old pains? What if God's hand wasn't pushing him down but guiding him to something he couldn't yet see, a light he'd never dared to seek? For the first time, the thought stirred something quiet and almost steady within him—a notion that maybe, just maybe, there was a reason he hadn't seen before.

Romans 5:3-4 (NIV) says:

"Not only so, but we also glory in our sufferings, because we know that suffering produces perseverance; perseverance, character; and character, hope."

David's fingers hovered over the screen of his phone. The last text he'd sent to Sandi still stared back at him, unanswered, the words hanging in the air between them like the weight of a thousand unspoken things.

"Baby, please. Come back. We can work it out, I promise. It's not too late. You know we have something special. I miss you so much."

He had sent it hours ago. There had been no reply, nothing but the familiar, hollow silence. The silence that felt like a betrayal, but also like a warning. A message he wasn't ready to hear.

He stared at the screen, his mind replaying the same scene over and over. Her face, so beautiful when he first met her, now unrecognizable, worn out by the life she was living. It was hard to even picture her anymore without the haze of K-2, the so-called synthetic marijuana, clouding everything she once was. K-2 was more like a plague sent by none other than Satan himself, David mused.

Sandi had become a shell of herself, lost in the addiction that consumed her. She was willing to sell herself for the synthetic high, something that was more important to her than food and water—more important than life itself. More important than him.

David swallowed hard, a lump forming in his throat. He couldn't even remember when she started needing it more than him, but it was obvious now. Every time they talked, every time she slipped further, he could see the woman he once knew slipping away into the fog of her addiction. It hurt. More than he could put into words.

But David still missed her. Deeply.

His mind kept replaying the good times, the warmth, the way she made him feel like the world was right when everything else seemed so wrong. He'd do anything to go back to those moments, to fix everything.

But he couldn't fix her. Not when she was so far gone.

With trembling hands, he put the phone down. There were no more words. No more texts. Just emptiness.

The memory hit David like a sledgehammer, raw and unforgiving. He was walking through the dark corridors of his mind, drawn back to that day, the second week back in Corpus Christi.

TRAP HOUSE

The house smelled of stale smoke and something stronger—something that David couldn't quite place but knew all too well. The walls were thin, cracked, and the floor was sticky from spilled liquor and the remnants of too many nights spent wasted. The living room was packed with people, all of them caught up in their own fog of drugs and desperation.

Sandi had been quiet that day, more so than usual. But he knew why. She had been off K-2 for months, five months to be exact. And now, here they were, back in Corpus Christi, homeless once again, staying in a place that felt more like a trap house than a home. They were both in a familiar place, but this time, it was different. She was struggling, fighting the urge to escape her own thoughts, her own fears.

And so, when the old habit crept back in, Sandi had made a choice that she would regret—at least, that's what David thought in the moment.

"It's just for a little while," she had said, her eyes pleading with him, as though the weight of the world rested on her shoulders. "It's the only way I can cope right now, David. I need it. I can't handle this stress. I can't think straight."

He should've argued with her. He should've seen the danger in her eyes, in the way her voice trembled with the lies she told herself. But instead, he nodded, because he knew the kind of pain she was in, the kind of brokenness she was carrying.

She lit the joint, her hands shaking. For a second, she looked like the woman he first fell in love with—the one who used to make him laugh, the one who used to light up every room she walked into. But the warmth didn't last long.

She took a couple of deep hits, and that's when it happened.

It was like a switch had been flipped, the way her body went stiff. Her eyes rolled back in her head, and her lips turned blue. David watched in horror as she collapsed, her body writhing in a violent seizure, her limbs jerking uncontrollably on the filthy floor.

The people in the room barely noticed. They were too caught up in their own highs, too numb to care about the woman who had just lost herself completely. But David couldn't ignore it. He couldn't walk away, no matter how broken he was inside.

He fell to his knees beside her, panic rising in his chest, his heart hammering in his ears. He could barely hear the muffled sounds of people talking, the distant laughter, the heavy beat of a stereo in the corner. Everything felt distant except for her.

"Baby, come on," he whispered, his voice shaking, as he held her in his arms. "Stay with me. Please, stay with me." David said a silent prayer, pleading to God on her behalf.

The paramedics arrived just as the seizure began to subside, and they rushed in to take over, pulling Sandi away from him. But David was frozen, unable to move, unable to even breathe. The fear in his chest tightened as the ambulance doors slammed shut behind them.

David stood there in the fading glow of the dim porch light, his mind reeling as the ambulance drove off. The sound of the sirens echoed in his chest, a constant reminder of the terror that had unfolded in that trap house. He had always known the drugs were slowly consuming Sandi, but seeing her like that—so vulnerable, so far gone—it felt like the universe had just ripped his heart out. She was slipping away, and there was nothing he could do to stop it.

He stood frozen for a long moment, unable to tear himself away from the spot. His body felt heavy, like the weight of the world had been placed on his shoulders.

The people inside the house had long since returned to their haze of numbness. No one asked what had happened to Sandi, no one seemed to care. But David could barely see straight, his vision blurry with the reality of it all. This wasn't just a phase. This wasn't just a slip-up. Sandi was drowning, and the drugs were her lifeline. The only thing that mattered to her was the next hit, the next high, the escape.

David's thoughts were interrupted by a voice from behind him.

"Man, you good?" It was a guy he barely knew, someone who'd been around during the chaos of the night, but had kept to himself.

David nodded without looking at him. "Yeah. She's going to be fine."

The guy didn't press, just nodded, and walked back into the house. But David couldn't shake the image of Sandi's lifeless body twitching on the floor.

He turned and stumbled down the sidewalk, unsure of where he was going. He didn't know how much time had passed—minutes, hours—it didn't matter. What mattered was that Sandi was gone, lost to the drugs, lost to the darkness that had consumed her. She had always been there for him, at least at the start, but now she was lost in the grip of addiction. And David...he was powerless to save her. David eventually found her at the county hospital. Sandi promising not to use again, David hearing the lies in her voice only nodded.

Spiral Out (The Present)

He thought back to the early days when they first came together in Houston. It felt like a lifetime ago, the way she made him feel like he was someone worth loving, worth believing in. Those were the days when he thought maybe they could escape the nightmare they had both been trapped in for so long. But the darkness had always been there, lurking beneath the surface, waiting to take over when they were least prepared.

Now, nine months later he was left with nothing. His car was gone. His job was gone. Sandi was gone. And his own soul felt as though it was slipping through his fingers, piece by piece.

David didn't even know how long he'd been walking. The city streets seemed to stretch on forever, endless and empty. But something inside of him snapped. He couldn't do this anymore. He couldn't keep chasing after someone who didn't want saving. He couldn't keep trying to patch up the broken pieces of his life when he didn't even know who he was anymore.

He had to leave.

But where could he go? How could he go on when all he had was the ghost of a woman who no longer existed?

David knew he had to break free from it all, from the addiction, from the pain, from the suffocating hold that Sandi had on his heart. But the struggle wasn't over.

The addiction was still there, inside him, whispering promises of relief that only led to more torment.

David stood still in the empty street, the echoes of the sirens fading into the distance. His chest ached, his mind a swirl of confusion and despair. But one thing was clear—he couldn't keep going like this. Not with Sandi, not with the drugs, and not with the endless spiral he'd been trapped in for so long.

He turned away from the scene, leaving the wreckage behind him. There was nothing more he could do for Sandi—not now, not anymore. He had to face the truth: she had chosen the drugs over him, and no amount of love or sacrifice could change that.

The weight of it all hit him hard. The years of struggles, the back-and-forth between hope and despair, the feeling of being lost in a world that didn't seem to care.

David had been running from himself, from his past, from everything that had hurt him. And now, with nothing left, he had nowhere else to go but forward.

But where was forward?

The Sound of Inevitability

His phone buzzed in his pocket, pulling him out of his spiral. It was a message from Eddy, one of the two true friends he had left in the world, someone who had tried to reach out to him for months now. He opened the message with hesitation.

"Man, you good? It's time. I got a place for you up here in Colorado. It's a fresh start. Let's do this."

David stared at the screen for a moment, the weight of Eddy's words sinking in. He had been avoiding this. The idea of leaving Texas, of starting over again, had felt impossible. But now, in this moment of raw clarity, it felt like his only option. He had nothing left here. No car, no home, no Sandi. Just a broken heart and a soul heavy with guilt.

Maybe it was time to take that first step forward. Maybe Colorado was the fresh start he so desperately needed.

He tapped out a quick reply.

"I'm coming."

David didn't know what awaited him there. He didn't know if it would be better, or if it would be just another dead end. But he couldn't stay here, not anymore. The memories, the pain, the addiction—they would follow him, no matter where he went. But maybe, just maybe, getting away would give him the space to heal.

He stuffed the phone back into his pocket and took a deep breath. He had a bus to catch. And as he walked away from the wreckage of his past, something inside him stirred—a flicker of hope, faint but real.

For the first time in a long while, David felt the faintest trace of something he hadn't felt in years: possibility.

Giving Up Things
That No Longer
Serve You

David felt a familiar tug in the pit of his stomach—the "old man" inside him, the voice that always whispered right when he was about to leave something behind. It urged him to get one last bag of meth before he hit the road. He tried to shrug it off, reasoning with himself: Once I get to Denver, I won't need it. I'll be done. It's over. Besides, Eddy won't have that stuff around, and I wouldn't even know where to find it. With that thought David walked into the restroom and before he could talk himself out of it, he tore open the last little bag Crystal had left him and flushed it down the toilet. The act gave him a fleeting sense of liberation.

But the voice persisted, playing on his doubt, on his need to hang on to something familiar. As he walked, memories surfaced of the last time he'd almost lost everything—more than just his freedom, but his life.

It was almost three years ago now. David had been cruising down a backroad, on edge after two days without sleep. His mind was buzzing, drowsy but wired.

When he spotted the red and blue lights flashing behind him, a wave of panic shot through him. His heart pounded; his mind raced. There it was in his pocket—an ounce of meth. He knew what it meant if they found it on him: prison. The thought alone chilled him to the core, the cold, endless nights, the walls closing in, the way time dragged in that place. He couldn't go back.

Without thinking, he did the only thing that came to mind. He fished the bag from his pocket, ripped it open, and before he could second-guess himself, shoved the whole thing into his mouth. He chewed, wincing as the bitter crystals crunched between his teeth, stinging his tongue, scraping his gums. He barely kept himself from gagging. Just get through this, he told himself. Once they're gone, I'll puke it up.

When the cop finally let him go with a warning, David pulled over and tried everything to bring the stuff back up. But it wouldn't come out. He tried until his throat burned, but nothing. Soon, the effects started to hit him, and they hit hard. The world around him spun, colors blurred. His heart pounded so hard; he thought it might burst. He called the only person he thought would nowhere to find him, his little brother Sean.

SECOND CHANCES

David didn't remember much after that—only waking up days later in the hospital, his little brother Sean beside him, face drawn with worry. The doctors told him he'd barely made it. An overdose of that scale had almost been the end of him, shutting down his lungs and heart, leaving him in a coma for three days. It was a miracle, they'd said. A miracle he didn't deserve, David often thought. But here he was, still breathing, still fighting the same fight.

This stuff isn't what it used to be; he told himself. The high doesn't even work anymore. But still, the old man in him clung to it, just for a while longer.

As David wrestled with the decision, he felt that nagging pull again, the urge to grab one last bag, to escape just a little longer. He knew he was on the verge of leaving his old life behind, stepping onto that bus to Denver and into the unknown. Yet the temptation still clawed at him, refusing to loosen its grip.

To everything there is a season, and a time to every purpose under the heaven...

The words echoed in his mind, slow and haunting, as if spoken by some voice deep within. A time to be born, and a time to die; a time to plant, and a time to harvest. He repeated the lines under his breath, almost like a chant, trying to let them wash over the doubt in his heart.

Some part of him knew he'd been running from this moment, avoiding the truth that this was, indeed, a time to let go. Meth had become a lifeline when everything else had shattered—his family, his freedom, Sandi. The high dulled his regrets, numbed his guilt, took the edge off his pain. But as he stood there, on the cusp of something new, he wondered if it was time to plant something different, to allow a new life to root itself in him, one not consumed by the cycle of highs and lows that had kept him bound.

David's hand lingered in his pocket, grasping at nothing but empty space. It was the season to leave this behind, to allow himself the hope, however small, that things could change. And as the dawn broke through the clouds, he finally took a deep breath, letting go of that last fleeting urge.

Without thinking anymore, before the doubts could work their way in, David got up and practically bolted toward the door. He knew how it worked—how his own mind would wear him down, piece by piece, like a tireless prosecutor. You'll never change. Who are you trying to fool? You think you're worth saving? He knew he could talk himself out of anything if given the chance.

The doubts whispered like ghosts; each one cloaked in familiarity. Who knows you better than me? He could almost feel them smirking, daring him to believe in something greater than this endless cycle. How could God ever use someone like you? The thought stung, hard. To work miracles, to bring light into darkness, to be some beacon of hope?

He pushed those voices down, each one fainter as he picked up his pace. The sky above had brightened, morning spilling its first golden rays over the city. David barely noticed; his eyes were set on the road ahead, his steps quick, his resolve solidifying with every stride. He was going to that bus station, no turning back.

David pushed through his doubts as he left, the last shred of hesitation lingering. Heading toward the bus station, he knew he couldn't just leave without seeing Gee Bee, his dog. She'd been his one constant through it all, his loyal companion through rough nights and dead-end days.

The Dog That Waited

When Sandi had arranged for a friend to keep her while David was in jail, it had relieved him a bit, knowing she'd be safe, at least for now. He only hoped she'd understand when he told her he'd be back, that he'd return with something better—a real home.

As David called out, "Gee Bee!" her head popped out from under the shade of the house, her ears perking up at the sound of his voice. Within moments, she was bounding toward him, her paws kicking up small clouds of dust. The sight of her brought back a flood of memories —how small she'd been when he first saw her, a little bundle of black and brown fur with those wide, innocent eyes.

It felt like ages ago when Sandi had started begging him for a puppy. "I wanna puppy, David I want one so bad..." she'd say, over and over, until it wore him down.

He knew it wasn't right; they barely had enough for themselves, and life was already hard enough without the responsibility of a pet. But Sandi had been in a dark place, and he'd wanted to see her smile, to lift her spirits even a little. So, against his better judgment, he gave in, and they got Gee Bee.

At first, Gee Bee was "their" dog, but she'd slowly taken to David, curling up close to him, following him around wherever he went. She had a way of sensing when he was feeling low, pressing her nose into his hand as if to say, "I'm here." Sandi noticed and didn't like it—she'd accuse David of stealing her dog, especially when they argued, saying, "Well, she's your dog now!"

But Gee Bee didn't care about their spats. She'd chosen David as her person, she loved Sandi too, but she had a different bond with David. Now, as she leaped into his arms, her wagging tail smacking against his leg, he felt a familiar pang. Leaving her was the hardest part of this good-bye, but he looked her in the eyes and whispered, "I'll be back for you, girl. I promise."

ROADS LESS TRAVELED

David stepped onto the Greyhound bus, his backpack slung over one shoulder, finding a seat near the back. He took a deep breath as the bus pulled away, leaving behind everything familiar yet fractured. He remembered Proverbs 16:9: "A man's heart deviseth his way: but the Lord directeth his steps." The verse echoed in his mind, giving him some comfort that maybe, just maybe, he was on the right path, even if he couldn't see what lay ahead.

As the city slowly faded into the background, David settled in, eyes tracing the landscape outside. The road stretched out before him, long and winding, and each mile brought a sense of both relief and unease. For the first time in years, he felt like he was moving toward something greater than the endless cycle he'd been stuck in.

The bus rolled into a small town for the first layover, a dusty place in the middle of nowhere. David wandered around the bus terminal, stretching his legs and grabbing a vending machine snack. He noticed an elderly man with a worn-out Bible in his lap, nodding off. When the man caught him looking, he opened his eyes and smiled.

"You headed far?" the man asked, a glimmer of wisdom in his gaze.

"Colorado," David replied, not sure how much to share.

The man nodded approvingly. "I'm just headed to the next town over. But son, wherever you're going, remember—God's got you on this path. Even the bumps along the way are part of His plan."

David sat with that for a moment, feeling a strange warmth. He hadn't opened up to anyone in so long, but this stranger's words felt like a gift. As the bus prepared to board, the old man patted David's shoulder. "Safe travels, son," he said before settling into his seat.

The next stretch of road took David through vast, open fields and small towns that seemed untouched by time. Occasionally, the bus would pass broken-down barns and grazing cattle, scenes that felt oddly peaceful to him. The monotony was broken by a quick layover in a town where he met a young woman with a guitar slung over her shoulder. Her fingers were calloused, her clothes simple, yet she had an energy about her that was contagious. She noticed him glancing at her guitar.

"Play?" she asked, nodding toward the instrument.

"Used to," David admitted with a shrug.

Without hesitation, she handed it over, her eyes bright with encouragement. Tentatively, he strummed a few chords, the music feeling both familiar and foreign under his fingers. She watched, smiling. "Sometimes, we've got to play our way through the tough times," she said. "Good luck out there."

David returned the guitar and nodded his thanks, feeling strangely lighter as he boarded the bus once again. There was something about these chance encounters that made him feel like maybe he was shedding old parts of himself with each mile.

Somewhere between Texas and Colorado, he pulled out his phone and texted Crystal.

Hey. I'm on my way to Denver. Decided it's time for a change. Thanks for everything... take care of yourself, alright?

A few minutes later, her response pinged back.

Denver? Good for you, David. Don't be a stranger. And stay safe.

COLORADO

The landscapes began to change as the bus neared the state line. Rolling hills gave way to flatter stretches of desert, and finally, in the distance, he saw the faint outline of the Rockies, rugged and sharp against the sky. As the bus wound closer, he found himself captivated by the sight of Cheyenne Mountain, looming larger and more imposing with each mile.

David pressed his face to the glass, drinking it all in—the sheer enormity of the mountain, its snow-capped peak stretching high above the clouds. He'd never seen anything like it. For a moment, he forgot everything—forgot the bus, forgot his troubles. All that mattered was the sight before him, a glimpse of something unyielding and ancient. Also, with many conspiracies tied around it, but that was something to ponder at a later time.

Something deep within him stirred. Maybe this was what he'd been chasing all along: the sense of awe, of beauty untouched by the chaos of his own life.

As David watched the mountain recede in the distance and the bus entered the outskirts of Denver, his thoughts drifted back to the words he'd heard in the small terminal from that old man. It was a strange feeling—he'd been on the run, or at least running in place, for so long. But now, somewhere inside, he was beginning to feel a glimmer of purpose. Maybe this trip was more than just a way out. Maybe he really was being guided, even if he couldn't see the full picture yet.

He reached into his backpack and pulled out a small, worn Bible Crystal had given him years ago. Flipping it open, almost at random, his eyes landed on Jeremiah 29:11: "For I know the plans I have for you, declares the Lord, plans to prosper you and not to harm you, plans to give you hope and a future."

The words washed over him like a balm. He thought about everything he'd lost—the car, Gee Bee, Sandi. So many pieces of his life scattered and broken, yet here was this promise, this assurance that his life wasn't a mistake or a mess to be abandoned. There was a plan in it, a hope he couldn't fully grasp yet but that maybe was there all along, hidden just beneath the rubble.

David tucked the Bible away, leaning his head back against the seat and closing his eyes. For the first time in months, he felt something lift within him—a quiet, cautious peace. A sense that his journey to Colorado, this fresh start, might really be the beginning of something he'd never dared imagine for himself.

As the bus finally pulled into the Denver station, David took a deep breath, stepped off, and felt the crisp mountain air filling his lungs.

As David stepped off the bus and felt the mountain air hit him, he was struck by an overwhelming sense of both excitement and fear. Everything was new and uncertain, and for a moment, he felt his pulse quicken, questions bubbling up in his mind. What if this doesn't work out? What if I can't make a fresh start here?

But then, just as quickly, he felt something else—a nudge, a steadying whisper within, echoing a verse he'd learned long ago but had almost forgotten, Proverbs 3:5-6: "Trust in the Lord with all your heart and lean not on your own understanding; in all your ways submit to him, and he will make your paths straight."

The words seemed to resonate deeply, reaching places in his heart that had long been hardened by doubt. He knew how much he relied on his own instincts, his own reasoning, and how often that had left him lost and empty. Standing there, breathing in that mountain air, he felt a gentle challenge to finally let go of his need to control everything, to let the divine plan unfold without trying to force his own version of it.

As he walked away from the bus terminal, those words stayed with him. Trust...submit...he will make your paths straight. For the first time, David felt the weight of his own uncertainty begin to lift, replaced by a quiet assurance that even though he didn't know what was next, he didn't have to. There was a greater path laid out before him—one he was just beginning to discover.

As David moved through the streets of Denver, his body and mind felt the toll of all he'd been through—the sleepless nights, endless anxieties, and scars he carried from so many years of struggle. His limp grew worse, and his joints ached in the dry mountain air. He felt worn down, like his spirit was barely holding together.

Yet, as he looked up at the towering mountains beyond the city, a new thought came to him—one that hadn't surfaced in a long time. Jeremiah 30:17: "For I will restore health to you, and your wounds I will heal, declares the Lord."

The words struck him in a way he hadn't expected, almost as though he was hearing them for the first time. It was a promise—a glimpse of something he had barely dared to hope for. Could there really be restoration, even after everything he'd been through? After all the wounds he'd inflicted on himself, all the pain he'd absorbed from others, could healing be possible?

David took a deep breath, letting the words sink in. For years he'd numbed himself, tried to patch over the pain, but nothing had truly healed. Standing there, feeling the weight of his past fall heavy on him, he realized this promise was what he needed most. Real healing wouldn't come from anything external—it would come from within, from something greater than himself.

With that in mind, David took his first step forward, ready to begin the path to a new kind of recovery—one that was as much spiritual as it was physical. The ache in his body didn't vanish, but somehow, it felt a little less burdensome, like there was a deeper strength carrying him forward.

Reunion at Union Station

Downtown Denver buzzed with life, its crisp November air carrying the scent of roasted coffee and faint diesel fumes. The towering buildings seemed to lean into one another like old friends, and the imposing Rockies loomed in the distance, silent witnesses to his arrival.

Union Station came into view, its grand, historic façade a stark contrast to the life David had been leading. He hesitated for a moment, the words of Jeremiah 30:17 echoing in his mind: "For I will restore health to you, and your wounds I will heal, declares the Lord."

As David rounded the corner, the sight of Union Station stopped him in his tracks. The brass clock above the entrance gleamed in the late afternoon sun, its ornate hands marking the hour with quiet precision. The glass doors reflected his scruffy appearance—threadbare jacket, worn-out backpack slung over one shoulder, and exhaustion etched into his face. Around him, polished travelers wheeled their luggage across the cobblestone path, oblivious to the contrast he brought to the scene.

The rhythmic clatter of rolling suitcases blended with snippets of laughter and hurried footsteps, creating a lively, almost musical backdrop. Nearby, a street performer strummed a soulful tune on his guitar, his weathered hat resting on the ground with a scattering of loose change inside.

David adjusted his backpack, the rough strap digging into his shoulder. The cool Denver air nipped at his cheeks, sharp and invigorating after hours confined on the bus. He took a deep breath. The earthy scent of fallen leaves mixed with the faint metallic tang of approaching snow, filling his lungs and clearing his head.

The station itself was a blend of history and modernity—marble floors and high arched ceilings, softened by the warm glow of pendant lights. The smell of fresh-baked pastries wafted from a nearby café, an inviting aroma that contrasted with the faint traces of engine grease and exhaust lingering from the bus depot.

David swallowed against the dryness in his mouth, the lingering bitterness of the cheap coffee he'd had at his last layover still clinging to his tongue. A gust of wind blew through the street, and he pulled his jacket tighter around himself, his heart pounding with anticipation.

As he neared the entrance, he saw him—Eddy. The years hadn't changed Eddy's unmistakable stance, though his hair was longer now, and his frame carried a bit more weight. Their eyes met, and Eddy broke into a grin, his arms opening wide as he called out, "David!"

The sound of Eddy's voice brought a wave of familiarity, both comforting and surreal. David quickened his step, and when Eddy clasped his hand in a firm shake before pulling him into a hug, the warmth of the gesture cut through the chill. For a moment, David felt anchored, as if he'd finally reached the shore after years lost at sea.

"Welcome to Denver, brother," Eddy said, his voice filled with a sincerity David hadn't heard in a long time.

David glanced around, taking in the bustling energy of Union Station. This was it. The beginning of something new.

Catching Up

The air inside Union Station carried the aroma of freshly brewed coffee mingled with the faint tang of baked goods. David followed Eddy into one of the station's cozy coffee shops. The polished wooden floors creaked slightly under their feet as they approached the counter. A chalkboard menu displayed a variety of drinks in elaborate cursive, and soft jazz played in the background, blending with the hum of conversations and the occasional hiss of the espresso machine.

Eddy glanced over his shoulder; his expression casual but warm. "What'll it be? My treat."

David hesitated. "Just a black coffee. Straightforward."

Eddy raised a brow. "Still the same David. Always keeping it simple."

After ordering, they found a small table near the window, where sunlight streamed in and cast long shadows across their cups. David cradled his coffee, feeling the heat seep into his palms. He stared into the dark liquid, as though the swirling steam might hold answers to questions, he couldn't yet articulate.

Eddy broke the silence first. "Man, it's been a long time. You look... different. Life been rough on you?"

David chuckled dryly, taking a sip of his coffee. "That's an understatement. But yeah, you could say it's been a rollercoaster. How about you? What brought you out here to Colorado?"

Eddy leaned back, his hands resting on the sides of his coffee cup. "The mountains, mostly, and work. Needed a fresh start after... well, a lot of things. I won't lie to you, though. It hasn't been all sunshine and rainbows. But being here, it's given me perspective, you know?"

David nodded slowly. "I get that. Perspective is something I've been trying to find myself. Feels like I've spent my whole life running from one fire to the next, trying not to get burned."

Eddy gave him a long look, the kind that seemed to weigh a person's soul. "You're here now, though. That's a start. And I'll tell you this— Denver isn't the easiest place to start over, but if you're serious about it, I'll help you however I can."

David felt a lump rise in his throat. He stared out the window, where the city seemed alive with possibility. "I appreciate that, Eddy. More than you know."

Eddy smiled, a faint gleam of hope in his eyes. "Well, let's see where this journey takes us. I've got a feeling it's gonna be a hell of a ride."

They clinked their coffee cups together like glasses of champagne, an unspoken pact sealed in that moment.

On the Road to Eddy's Place

David eased into the passenger seat of Eddy's new Toyota SUV, a sleek vehicle with a clean interior that still smelled faintly of factory leather. The rumble of the engine hummed in the background as they navigated the busy streets of downtown Denver, leaving Union Station behind.

Eddy tapped his fingers on the steering wheel, a faint smile on his face. "Man, I gotta say, it's good to see you again, David. Life's taken some strange turns for me since we last crossed paths."

David glanced at him, intrigued. "Yeah? Like what?"

Eddy chuckled, his eyes crinkling at the corners. "You wouldn't believe half of it if I told you. But I'll try anyway. You remember when I got out of prison? I decided to take a leap of faith. On a whim, I packed up everything I owned—which wasn't much—and bought a one-way ticket to Alaska. I'd always wanted to see the place, you know? But it was more than that. I was searching for something, even if I didn't know exactly what it was."

David raised an eyebrow, curious. "Alaska, huh? That's a hell of a place to start over, seems kinda extreme. What'd you do up there?"

Eddy smiled; his gaze distant as he recalled those years. "I ended up staying for seven years. Worked on fishing boats at first, then got into carpentry. But it wasn't just about the work. There's something about that place, David. The vastness of it. The quiet. I'd sit out under the northern lights and feel like the universe was speaking to me. It's hard to explain, but it felt like God was leaving me little breadcrumbs to follow."

David frowned slightly, leaning back in his seat. "Breadcrumbs?"

"Yeah," Eddy said, his tone thoughtful. "Little signs, little nudges. Like one time, I was hiking through the woods, completely lost, and I stumbled on this tiny, weathered chapel in the middle of nowhere. No one was there, but I felt this overwhelming peace, like I was meant to find it. I'd been questioning everything at that point—my past, my purpose—and then there it was, this symbol of hope, just waiting for me. Stuff like that kept happening. I started keeping a journal to write it all down. It was like God was whispering, 'Keep going.'"

David stared out the window at the Denver skyline, trying to picture Eddy in the frozen wilderness of Alaska, finding himself. "That's... heavy, man. So, what brought you back down south?"

"Well," Eddy said, his smile widening, "after Alaska, I felt this pull to give back. So, I spent some time in Mexico as a missionary, helping build houses for families who had nothing. It was humbling, man. Seeing those kids smile even though they had so little? It changed me. Made me realize how much I'd taken for granted.

Then, a few years ago, I went to Jerusalem."

"Jerusalem?" David echoed; his voice tinged with awe.

Eddy nodded; his eyes gleaming with the memory. "That was the pinnacle, David. Walking where Jesus walked, standing at the Western Wall, the Garden of Gethsemane... it was like the Bible came alive. There was one moment I'll never forget. I was standing on the Mount of Olives, looking out over the city, and this gust of wind came out of nowhere. It wasn't like a normal breeze—it felt alive, like it carried something with it. I can't explain it, but I knew in my bones it was God

telling me, 'This is your path.'"

David sat in silence, taking it all in. "So, what brought you to Denver?"

Eddy grinned. "That's the craziest part. Remember that guy, Rico? We were locked up with him for a while."

David's brow furrowed in thought. "Rico... yeah, I remember. He was always talking about starting some big project when he got out."

"Well, he did," Eddy said. "He's running this recovery organization I work for. It's all about helping guys like us rebuild their lives. They hired me as a peer recovery coach. I help people dealing with addiction, getting out of prison, or just trying to find their way. It's wild, David. I get paid to do what I love—helping people. And it feels like every part of my journey led me here.

Alaska, Mexico, Jerusalem—it all connected somehow. Like God was shaping me for this, even when I didn't realize it. Jeremiah 29:11, man: 'For I know the plans I have for you,' declares the Lord, 'plans to prosper you and not to harm you, plans to give you hope and a future.' I didn't get it back then, but now it all makes sense."

David stared at Eddy, amazed. He'd never heard him talk like this before. There was a conviction in his voice, a fire in his eyes that wasn't there twenty years ago.

It was inspiring, but also intimidating.

"That's incredible," David said finally. "I mean, you've done all this stuff, had all these experiences... Meanwhile, I've just been surviving, man. Scraping by, making the same mistakes over and over."

Eddy glanced at him, his expression softening. "Don't do that, David. Don't compare your path to mine; comparison is the thief of joy. Gods got something for you too. You're here now, aren't you? That's no accident. Trust me, your story's just getting started."

They drove on in silence for a while, the city giving way to open highway. The mountains loomed in the distance, their snow-capped peaks glowing in the late afternoon sun. David couldn't take his eyes off them.

"You've never seen mountains before, have you?" Eddy asked, noticing David's gaze.

"Not like this," David admitted. "Pictures don't do them justice. They're... massive. Like they're alive or something."

"They are," Eddy said with a grin. "Well, not literally, but they have a way of making you feel small in the best possible way. Like a reminder that the world's bigger than your problems."

David nodded, still transfixed. The sight stirred something in him—a mixture of awe and hope, like the mountains were a promise of something new, something better.

"So, what's the plan now?" Eddy asked, pulling him back to the moment.

David tore his eyes from the window. "Honestly? I don't know. I'm just trying to figure things out one step at a time."

"That's all you need to do," Eddy said. "One step at a time. And remember Proverbs 3:5-6: 'Trust in the Lord with all your heart and lean not on your own understanding; in all your ways submit to Him, and He will make your paths straight.' You're not alone in this, David. You've got me. And you've got Him, whether you realize it yet or not."

David didn't respond, but the words lingered. For the first time in a long time, he felt a flicker of something he thought he'd lost—hope.

Eddy told David about a place he thought could really help. "There's this place called the New Life Rescue Mission," Eddy began as they drove along. "They run this program called HOPE (Helping Others Provides Eternal-life.) It's an 11-month Christian-based program for people who are homeless or just need a fresh start. It's serious, though. You've gotta stay clean and sober, and they'll test you to make sure. But if you stick with it, it can change your life. They teach you job skills, help you build a résumé, even set you up to go back to school or learn a trade. It's not easy, but it's worth it."

David looked at him skeptically. "That sounds... intense. Eleven months is a long time."

"It is," Eddy admitted. "But think about it—what's eleven months compared to the rest of your life? This could be the break you've been praying for, man. A chance to get things straight, to figure out who you are without all the... chaos."

David stared out the window, the mountains still looming on the horizon. He didn't know what to say. It sounded good—too good, maybe—but it also sounded terrifying. The idea of committing to something like that, of stripping everything down and starting over, was almost too much to wrap his head around.

Eddy didn't push. He let the conversation settle as they drove through the city. Eventually, he shifted gears. "Listen, I've got a little place you can crash for a few days while you think about it. I take care of this old church for a lady I know—kind of a live-in gig. There's a little space upstairs where you can lay low. It's nothing fancy, but it's quiet, and it'll give you time to figure out your next move."

"Thanks, man," David said quietly. "I appreciate it."

"Don't mention it," Eddy replied. "We've all needed a hand at some point. Just paying it forward."

The church was small and unassuming, tucked away on a quiet street. As they pulled up, David noticed its peeling paint and weathered stone, a sign of its age.

But there was something comforting about it, too—something solid, enduring.

Inside, Eddy showed David to the space upstairs. It was simple but clean—a small bed, a table, a lamp. "Make yourself at home," Eddy said. "We'll head to the Rescue Mission in a couple of days. I'll set you up with an interview and show you around."

David sat down on the bed, suddenly overwhelmed by everything. He hadn't felt this kind of stillness in years. For the first time, it seemed like there might actually be a way forward.

Before Eddy left, he turned to David with a reassuring smile. "Just think about it, okay? No pressure. But remember Jeremiah 30:17: 'I will restore you to health and heal your wounds,' declares the Lord. 'Because you are called an outcast, Zion for whom no one cares.' You're not an outcast, David. Not anymore. You've got people in your corner now. And God's got a plan for you—I promise."

David nodded, letting the words sink in. Maybe Eddy was right. Maybe this was his chance to start over, to heal, to finally find his way. For the first time in a long time, the idea didn't seem so impossible.

New Life Rescue Mission

David sat across from the admissions officer at the New Life Rescue Mission, nervously tapping his fingers on his knee. After several hours of interviews, forms, and waiting, the woman finally extended her hand with a smile. "Welcome to the HOPE Program, David. You're officially part of the Blue Team."

Relief flooded David's chest, though he wasn't entirely sure what being on the Blue Team meant. "Thank you," he said, shaking the woman's hand.

The admissions officer handed David a folder. "This is your care team," she explained. "You'll have a caseworker, a counselor, and a chaplain assigned to help you through the program. They'll guide you, check in with you regularly, and make sure you stay on track."

A woman knocked on the door and stepped inside. "This is Martha," the admissions officer said. "She'll be showing you around the facility and getting you settled."

David stood and followed Martha into the hallway, feeling both excited and apprehensive. As they walked, she explained more about the program. "We have a pretty structured routine here," she said. "You'll have daily classes, chores, and time for individual counseling and Bible study. It's not easy, but it's designed to help you rebuild your life."

They passed through a cafeteria filled with men sitting at long tables, eating and talking. The atmosphere was a mix of camaraderie and tension. "This is where you'll have meals," Martha said. "Three squares a day. You'll also have access to snacks in the evenings."

Next, she showed David the classrooms, the chapel, and the recreation area, which had a pool table and a few worn-out couches. Finally, she led him to a dormitory wing and stopped in front of a door.

"Here we are," she said, opening the door to reveal a modest room with two sets of bunk beds, a small window, and a private bathroom. Two men were sitting on one of the lower bunks, talking quietly. They both looked up when David entered, their expressions shifting from curiosity to mild annoyance.

"This is your new roommate, David," Martha announced cheerfully.

The taller of the two men sighed. "Another one? Man, this room is already cramped."

The other guy, shorter with a shaved head, muttered, "No kidding. Where's he even gonna put his stuff?"

David hesitated in the doorway, feeling the weight of their resentment. "Hey, I'll try not to be in your way," he said awkwardly.

Martha cleared her throat. "Let's try to make David feel welcome, okay? Remember, you were the new guy once, too."

The taller man shrugged. "Whatever. Top bunk's open."

David nodded and tossed his small bag onto the bed. "Thanks," he said, climbing up to inspect the thin mattress.

Before leaving, Martha gave him an encouraging smile. "Give it time," she whispered. "This is a big adjustment for everyone, but you'll find your place here."

After she left, David unpacked the few belongings he had: some clothes, a Bible, and a worn notebook. The room was tight, and he could understand the other guys' frustration, but he was grateful to have a roof over his head and a place to start fresh.

Later, as he lay on the hard mattress, staring at the ceiling, he reminded himself of Proverbs 3:5-6: "Trust in the Lord with all your heart and lean not on your own understanding; in all your ways submit to Him, and He will make your paths straight."

The path wasn't clear yet, but David resolved to trust that it would unfold in time.

For the first 37 days, David felt caged. The rules of the HOPE Program were strict: no leaving the facility, no contact with the outside world unless approved, and a rigid schedule that left little room for distraction. The facility itself, a repurposed old hotel, was both a blessing and a burden. Its narrow hallways, creaky floors, and peeling wallpaper reminded him of where he'd been, but the structured environment also gave him a sense of security and stability he hadn't felt in years.

With nowhere else to turn, David began to use his free time to explore things he'd never given much thought to before. During his assigned computer lab hours, he discovered a wealth of inspirational content on YouTube. One evening, as the sun dipped behind the urban skyline, he stumbled across a series of videos on Stoic philosophy.

The words of Marcus Aurelius, Epictetus, and Seneca struck a deep chord within him. Their teachings about controlling one's emotions, accepting hardships, and focusing on what could be controlled resonated with David's own struggles. He was captivated by the idea that suffering could be a teacher and that adversity was not a punishment but an opportunity to grow stronger.

In the weeks that followed, Stoic principles became a daily meditation for him. He'd repeat to himself phrases like, "You have power over your mind—not outside events. Realize this, and you will find strength." He began keeping a small journal where he noted reflections from his day, drawing parallels between the ancient teachings and his own life.

But it wasn't just philosophy that captured his attention. One day, as the algorithm guided him deeper into content on purpose and resilience, David stumbled upon videos discussing "God's chosen ones." It was a term he had never encountered before. Curious, he clicked on a video, and as he listened, he felt an uncanny familiarity in what the speaker described.

The video explained that chosen ones often face lives filled with struggle and hardship. They might endure broken homes, betrayals, rejection, and periods of wandering, but all of it served a divine purpose.

The speaker went on to describe how chosen ones often feel a deep sense of calling, even when they don't understand it. They're tested repeatedly but are meant to rise, becoming beacons of light for others.

David 's heart raced as he listened. Every word seemed to describe his life. His childhood trauma, the relentless setbacks, the sense of isolation he'd carried for so long—all of it suddenly felt like pieces of a larger puzzle. Could it be that his suffering wasn't random? That his life, full of pain and misdirection, had been preparing him for something greater?

Over the following days, David devoured every video he could find on the topic. The more he learned, the more convinced he became that this wasn't a coincidence. He reflected on moments in his past when he'd felt guided or protected, even in his darkest hours. He began to see his journey not as a series of failures but as a refining fire.

One night, as he sat on the edge of his bunk, the words of Jeremiah 29:11 came to him with renewed clarity: "For I know the plans I have for you, declares the Lord, plans to prosper you and not to harm you, plans to give you a hope and a future."

David closed his eyes and whispered, "Maybe... maybe there's more to me than I thought."

During David 's first two weeks at the HOPE Program, he encountered a host of unique personalities, each carrying their own stories, struggles, and perspectives.

Among them was a man named Scott, whose energy and passion were impossible to ignore. Scott, a wiry middle-aged man with piercing blue eyes and a beard that he often joked made him look like an Old Testament prophet, was a force of nature when it came to his beliefs.

Scott was outspoken—sometimes to a fault—about religion and the state of the world. Over meals in the cafeteria or during breaks in the common room, he'd passionately discuss how the government was hiding the truth from everyone. "They want us blind," he'd say, his voice rising as his hands gestured animatedly.

"The media, the politicians—they're all in on it. But the biggest lie? Aliens. They're not little green men; they're fallen angels!"

David listened with equal parts curiosity and skepticism. Scott's theories were colorful, to say the least, but his sincerity was undeniable. He was absolutely convinced that what most people thought of as UFOs or extraterrestrials were actually Satan's fallen angels masquerading as beings from another planet, deceiving humanity as part of a grand, diabolical scheme.

"They're preparing the world for the Antichrist," Scott insisted one afternoon as they sat outside during a rare moment of sun. "They'll come offering peace and advanced technology, but it's a trap. And mark my words, the end of the world as we know it is coming before this year is out."

At first glance, Scott might have seemed like a conspiracy theorist straight out of a late-night radio show, but David quickly realized that beneath his eccentric ideas was a deeply genuine an. Scott's fervent belief wasn't rooted in paranoia or fear; it stemmed from an unshakable conviction in God's Word and a desire to warn others about the spiritual warfare he believed was unfolding.

In one of their conversations, Scott quoted Ephesians 6:12: "For we do not wrestle against flesh and blood, but against the rulers, against the authorities, against the cosmic powers over this present darkness, against the spiritual forces of evil in the heavenly places." David had heard the verse before, but hearing it through Scott's lens gave it a new, almost tangible weight.

Scott's passion, while intense, also inspired David to dig deeper into his own beliefs. Was there truth to what Scott was saying? Or was Scott simply seeing patterns where none existed? Regardless, David found himself intrigued and began rereading Scripture with fresh eyes, looking for insights into the spiritual battles that might be at play.

One night, as David reflected on his conversations with Scott, he came across 2 Timothy 1:7: "For God gave us a spirit not of fear but of power and love and self-control." It struck him deeply. While Scott's warnings were sobering, David felt called to focus on the hope and strength that came from faith rather than the fear of what might come.

In the weeks that followed, Scott became a kind of sounding board for David, challenging him to think critically about the world and his place in it. While David didn't buy into all of Scott's theories, he couldn't deny that the man's zeal reignited a fire within him—a reminder that the world was full of unseen forces, both good and evil, and that staying grounded in faith was more important than ever.

THE CONVERSATION

In the common area, the room was buzzing with the usual mid-afternoon chatter, the clinking of trays, and the shuffle of footfalls. The smell of soup and stale bread lingered in the air, but it wasn't unpleasant. David sat at the long, worn wooden table in the HOPE Program's dining room. David, sitting across from Scott, tried to focus on his lunch but found his mind drifting. Scott, as usual, was animated—his eyes wide, his voice sharp as he leaned forward over his tray.

"You know, man, the government's been lying to us for decades. I mean, they hide everything. I'm telling you; it's all part of a bigger plan. They've been covering up the truth about the fallen angels—those aliens? They're the same thing. Demons, fallen angels, coming down here pretending to be something they're not. It's like... like a rehearsal for the final act."

David gave him a look, chewing slowly. He'd heard this before—Scott had a tendency to speak in apocalyptic terms, each conversation like it could be the last.

The idea that aliens were fallen angels seemed far-fetched, even absurd, but Scott's conviction was real. He wasn't just spouting nonsense—he truly believed this.

"And what's the final act?" David asked, curiosity creeping in despite his skepticism.

Scott leaned in closer, his eyes wide. "It's the end of days. But not in the way people think. It's coming soon. You can feel it in the air. I'm telling you, God's trying to wake us all up before it's too late. We're living in the last days, man."

David's brow furrowed. He wasn't sure if he believed in the same kind of "end of days" Scott saw, but there was something in the intensity of Scott's words that made him pause. There was a fire in his eyes—something David hadn't seen in a long time. Maybe it wasn't about aliens or conspiracies, but about something deeper: faith. A sense of purpose.

"Have you ever considered, like, maybe this end of days stuff... is more about our own lives, not some world catastrophe?" David asked, his voice quieter now, as he poked at the remnants of his food.

Scott's expression softened a little, though his passion remained. "What do you mean?"

David leaned back in his chair, feeling the weight of his words as he spoke. "I've been thinking a lot lately. I mean, you're all fired up about the end of the world, but maybe for some of us, the end of days is a personal thing. Like, we're living in our own end times. I don't know... maybe it's about facing our demons, breaking out of the darkness, finding redemption before it's too late for us personally."

Scott didn't say anything for a moment, his gaze shifting as if he were weighing David's words. Then he gave a small, almost reluctant nod. "I guess that makes sense, too." His voice had softened, and David could tell the wheels were turning in Scott's mind. "Maybe we're all a little stuck in our own end times, huh?"

David felt a surge of connection with him in that moment, something he didn't expect. Scott, for all his eccentricities, was seeking the same thing David was—truth.

"Well," David said, leaning forward slightly, "maybe the trick is figuring out where the end of your personal days is... and then living like you know the time's short.

Maybe that's when you really find out what you're meant to do, who you're meant to be."

Scott smiled, a slow grin that crept across his face. "Now you're talking, man. Now you're talking. That's what I'm saying. The world's a mess, but we've still got time. Time to get right with God... and maybe even save the world. If we don't wake up first, though, that's all she wrote."

David chuckled, though a small part of him couldn't shake the unsettling feeling that Scott wasn't entirely wrong. His words had weight, even if they didn't line up with everything David had ever believed. There was a hint of truth to the idea that time was fleeting and that finding purpose was urgent.

"Thanks for the talk, Scott," David said, nodding, the conversation stirring something deeper inside him.

"Anytime, man. Anytime," Scott replied, with that same wild-eyed energy. "We're all chosen ones in this fight. Gotta remembers that."

As David stood up to leave, he couldn't shake the feeling that Scott's chaotic worldview, his odd beliefs, and his urgency were all somehow connected to the greater journey ahead for him—whether he understood it now or not. Something about this place, this strange group of men, felt like it was all part of the divine plan. Just as he had felt in the past, when he had glimpsed that larger purpose, he now felt it again in the most unexpected way.

As he walked away from Scott, he couldn't help but think of the verse he had come across in his studies:

"For I know the plans I have for you," declares the Lord, "plans to prosper you and not to harm you, plans to give you a hope and a future." — Jeremiah 29:11

Maybe that's what this was about, he thought. Maybe he was finally finding the path that was meant for him.

Reflection on Destiny

A few days after their lunch conversation, David sat on the edge of his bed, staring out the small window of the room he shared with his two less-than-enthusiastic roommates. The late afternoon sunlight filtered in, casting long shadows across the walls. His Bible lay open on his lap, but his eyes weren't on the page. Instead, his mind kept drifting back to Scott.

Scott had gone on a passionate tangent the other day, talking about "angel numbers." Repeating sequences like 111 or 444, and 999, he said, were messages from God, guiding him along his path. At first, David had brushed it off as just another of Scott's eccentric beliefs, like the alien-demon conspiracy or his certainty about the end of days. But as Scott continued, recounting a series of seemingly improbable events—how he'd ended up in Mexico, how he'd met someone at just the right time to avoid disaster, how numbers seemed to appear when he needed reassurance—David couldn't help but feel a small, reluctant flicker of curiosity.

Scott's life sounded like a bizarre, real-world version of Forrest Gump, where everything happened to align perfectly, almost as if orchestrated by some unseen hand. It was hard not to wonder if there was something to it.

David shifted on the bed, rubbing his hand over his face. Was Scott crazy? Or was he onto something?

Maybe the real question was: could they both be onto something?

David's thoughts circled back to the concept of Chosen Ones, something he'd only recently learned about. He'd spent the past few nights diving into videos and articles about it. The idea was simple but profound—certain people were set apart by God, given extraordinary challenges and burdens to refine them for a greater purpose. The stories he'd read sounded a lot like his life: the hardship, the pain, the relentless feeling of being out of place in the world.

But if he was a Chosen One, what about Scott? What about some of the other people he'd met throughout his life, that just happened to be there when he needed a helping hand?

David leaned back against the wall, staring up at the ceiling. The idea that Scott was part of his "soul family" crept into his thoughts. It was something he'd heard about during one of his late-night YouTube spirals. Soul families were groups of people connected across lifetimes, bound together to help each other fulfill their divine missions. Could this be the reason God had guided him to this place, at this time? David had never put much stock in ideas like reincarnation or soul bonds, but lately, nothing seemed off the table.

What if Scott wasn't just some guy he'd met at the program? What if they were meant to meet?

David sat up and grabbed his journal from the nightstand. Writing had become a habit for him lately, a way to organize his thoughts. As he flipped to a blank page, he scrawled the words:

"Why did I meet Scott? What's the connection?"

The pen hovered over the page for a moment before he started writing again.

"Could it be that he's chosen too? Is he here to guide me, or am I here to guide him?"

David paused, chewing on the pen cap. A memory surfaced—something Scott had said during lunch.

"We're all chosen ones in this fight. Gotta remember that."

David had brushed it off at the time, but now, it felt like more than a throwaway comment. Maybe Scott didn't fully understand what he was saying, but he'd said it with such conviction that it stuck.

He flipped back a few pages in his Bible to a verse that had stood out to him earlier: "As iron sharpens iron, so one person sharpens another." **— Proverbs 27:17**

Maybe that was it. Maybe Scott and David had been brought together to sharpen each other, to prepare for something neither of them could yet see.

David closed the journal and leaned back again, his thoughts churning. The idea of being a Chosen One still felt too big, too heavy to fully embrace, but for the first time, he felt a spark of something close to belief.

And if Scott was part of this plan, this soul family... then maybe David wasn't as alone in this as he thought. Who else might he meet here that is part of this family.

For sure if anyone was part of his soul family it was Eddy...

Awakening to the Signs

Over the next week, David found himself caught in an uncanny wave of synchronicities. Scott's talk of angel numbers, synchronicities, and divine timing had planted seeds in his mind, but these experiences were watering them, urging them to grow.

It began with a familiar feeling—déjà vu. Not just the fleeting sense of familiarity everyone experiences now and then, but a deep, bone-chilling certainty that he'd already lived certain moments.

One evening, as he walked across the yard, David stopped mid-step, frozen by the overwhelming sensation that he had been here before. It was more than the repetition of routine; it was a memory etched into his soul. His thoughts flashed back to the night he met Jamie, how he'd told her, "I feel like we've done this before," and how she'd smiled, responding, "Maybe we have."

Now, that same feeling was happening more often, and it wasn't just during big moments. Sometimes, it was as simple as hearing someone's voice or catching a scent in the air. It was as if his soul was replaying fragments of a life, he wasn't fully aware of yet.

He'd been laying in his bed between classes one day with his eyes closed and suddenly he had a vision of a faulted ceiling with geometric patterns, and intricate stain glass windows emitting a soft cobalt blue into his vision, in his mind's eyes he could see this ceiling perfectly, and he heard faint harmonic notes in a sequence almost as if it were orchestrating the entire event. Well, it just so happened that the next day on a random whim they decided to stop at this beautiful church that Eddy had been wanting to see, and to Davids's astonishment when he walked through the front door and looked up, the exact same ceiling from his vision came into view. Standing there in awe of its magnificence and beauty, David barely realized that Eddy had already walked through the next set of doors into the main room where service is held. The inside was nothing short of breath taking, David began taking pictures on his phone, and though they were beautiful they fell short of the true glory of witnessing it firsthand.

As they were about to leave, they heard keys jingling, and someone coming up the stairs from a lower floor, followed by a greeting of," Hello" coming from the darkened stairs below. As the man came into view, David was taken aback. The man bore a striking resemblance to none other than Jesus of Nazareth. Of course, it wasn't Jesus but the director and caretaker of the church. Or was it, David thought and smiled to himself.

His name was Troy, who was very kind enough to give them a small tour of the community resource and meeting hall under the church. He also filled them in on some of the churches history, its patron, and the churches mission, which is to serve the homeless. David readily agreed to volunteer if they needed help.

It was a fascinating experience, and David wondered why God had given him the vision of this church yesterday, and what its significance was? David knelt and prayed before they left, giving thanks to God for all the wonders that were unfolding in his life.

Signs From the Universe

One afternoon, as David walked back from lunch, his thoughts scattered, he almost stepped on a small bird sitting in the middle of the sidewalk. Startled, he stopped and crouched down.

"What's wrong, little guy?" he murmured, reaching out cautiously.

To his surprise, the bird didn't flinch or flutter away. Instead, it tilted its head, allowing David to gently scoop it into his hands. It didn't appear to be injured, but its eyes were half-closed, fluttering open only occasionally.

David carried it to the back smoking area, cradling it in his hands as he sat down. He placed the bird gently in his cupped hand and lit a cigarette, watching it with quiet wonder.

"I don't know what to do for you," he said softly, "but you're safe for now."

He decided he'd take it upstairs and try to give it some water, but as if the bird heard him, it suddenly stood up in his hand. It hopped up his shirt and perched on his shoulder for a moment, looking around.

David chuckled. "You sure you're, okay?"

Without warning, the bird spread its wings and flew off, strong and steady. David watched it until it disappeared into the sky, a strange warmth blooming in his chest. He couldn't shake the feeling that the moment was more than coincidence.

KNOWING

The signs didn't stop there. One morning, David caught a ride with an Uber driver to a doctor's appointment. The woman, a friendly older lady with salt-and-pepper hair and an easy laugh, struck up a conversation.

People always seemed to open up to David even strangers. She was no different, telling him about her day, her family, and eventually mentioning that she was a Virgo.

David felt a spark of recognition. He couldn't explain why, but he just knew she'd have the same birthday as him.

"Let me guess," he said, grinning. "August 30th?"

The driver's mouth felt open. "How'd you know that?"

David shrugged, laughing. "Just a hunch."

As they continued talking, David couldn't shake the thought that the universe had nudged them together for a reason.

Unseen Nudges

Other signs came in quick, fleeting moments. One day, while reading his Bible in the courtyard, a gust of wind flipped the pages to **Isaiah 41:10**. The verse jumped out at him:

"Do not fear, for I am with you; do not be dismayed, for I am your God. I will strengthen you and help you; I will uphold you with my righteous right hand."

David read it three times, the words sinking deep into his soul. He couldn't explain why, but it felt like a direct message—comforting, reassuring, and undeniable.

Then there were the moments when he felt he already knew what someone was going to say before they said it. It wasn't all the time, but enough to notice. It wasn't déjà vu, but a knowing. Like when a staff member told him about a new rule, and he had already predicted the exact wording they'd use before they opened their mouth.

The Bigger Picture

These experiences began stacking up, pressing on David's skepticism. Scott's ramblings didn't seem so far-fetched anymore. It wasn't just angel numbers or theories about fallen angels—it was the undeniable feeling that David was part of something bigger.

David sat in his room one evening, flipping through his journal. He scribbled down each sign and experience, trying to make sense of them all.

"What are You trying to tell me?" he wrote, the question directed at the heavens.

He closed the journal and glanced at his reflection in the window. For the first time in a long time, he felt like he wasn't wandering aimlessly. Maybe Scott was right—maybe he was Chosen. Maybe he was finally starting to see the plan God had for him.

A Spiritual Awakening

Over the next week, David felt a shift within himself, something he couldn't ignore or rationalize away. It was as though the universe had been whispering to him for years, and now, in Colorado, it was finally speaking clearly.

Each day brought moments that left him in awe, moments he couldn't explain but felt deeply in his spirit. As he walked the halls of the HOPE Program facility, as he listened to the chaplain during morning devotionals, and even as he sat quietly smoking in the courtyard, David felt the undeniable presence of something greater.

He owed it all to Eddy, a man he hadn't seen in over two decades. Eddy, who'd been through his own spiritual rebirth, had not only offered David a place to stay but had also guided him to this exact moment in time.

"This isn't coincidence," David thought one evening, staring at the fading colors of the sunset from the facility's rooftop access. "This is God."

Conversations That Changed Everything

Eddy's words echoed in David's mind. The stories of his journey to Alaska, of building houses in Mexico, of standing on holy ground in Jerusalem — they weren't just tales of adventure. They were testimonies of faith, evidence of God's hand guiding Eddy's path.

"You know, David," Eddy had said during one of their late-night talks, "sometimes God uses people to pull us out of the dark. He sends people to show us the way, even if we don't realize it at the time. That's what happened to me, and now I think He's doing the same for you."

David had nodded, unsure of what to say. At the time, he wasn't convinced. But now, every fiber of his being told him Eddy was right.

MOMENTS OF CLARITY

One morning, during the program's Bible study, David came across **Jeremiah 29:11**:

"For I know the plans I have for you," declares the Lord, "plans to prosper you and not to harm you, plans to give you a hope and a future."

The verse hit him like a lightning bolt. He read it again, then a third time, the words sinking into his heart. It was as if God Himself were speaking to him directly, assuring him that every hardship, every wrong turn, had been part of a greater plan.

THE AWAKENING DEEPENS

David began to notice that his thoughts were changing. Where once he'd been consumed by bitterness, regret, and hopelessness, now he felt a glimmer of peace, a faint but growing sense of purpose.

In the quiet moments, he reflected on his life. The pain, the loss, the mistakes—they hadn't been meaningless. He saw now that they had shaped him, prepared him for this moment.

"This is my chance," he thought. "My chance to start over, to live the way I was meant to."

EDDY'S ROLE IN GOD'S PLAN

One evening, David pulled Eddy aside. They were sitting in the small church Eddy looked after, the dim light casting long shadows across the pews.

"Eddy," David began, his voice steady, "I don't know how to thank you for what you've done. Bringing me here, showing me this program —it's changed everything."

Eddy smiled; his eyes warm. "Don't thank me, brother. Thank God. I'm just the tool He used to get you here."

David nodded, swallowing the lump in his throat. "You've got no idea how much this means to me. I feel like... I don't know. Like I'm finally waking up."

"That's the Spirit working in you," Eddy said. "You're exactly where you're supposed to be, David. And this is just the beginning."

Renewed Hope

That night, David lay in his bed, staring at the ceiling. He thought about everything that had led him to this moment. The hardships, the failures, the people he'd lost—they all seemed to make sense now.

For the first time in years, David felt hope. Not the fleeting kind, but a deep, abiding hope that came from knowing he wasn't alone. God was with him, guiding him, just as He had guided Eddy.

"This is where my life starts over," David whispered to himself.

And in his heart, he knew it was true.

Opening Doors

David's growing interest in psilocybin mushrooms was born from a blend of curiosity and longing. He had read about their promising effects in alleviating depression, PTSD, and even providing terminal patients with a sense of peace. These stories ignited something deep inside him—a hope that perhaps this natural gift could serve as a gateway to his own spiritual and emotional healing.

His mind often drifted back to when he was fifteen, to those long summer afternoons with his best friend Martin. The two of them would wander the sprawling cow pastures around Victoria, Texas, gathering wild mushrooms. They didn't know much about the science back then, but they knew enough to recognize the bluish tint on the stems.

They weren't just tripping, though; it was something more. Every time they took mushrooms; Martin would inevitably start talking about God. At first, David had dismissed it as just a side effect of the drug, but soon he realized those conversations were different. They were intense, meaningful, and, strangely enough, grounding.

"Remember that time by the creek?" David thought to himself one night, lying in his bed. He recalled how Martin had talked about creation, the interconnectedness of life, and the idea that everything had a purpose. They were only teenagers, but those conversations felt bigger than them—like they were tapping into something ancient and profound.

The Calling to Psilocybin

Now, years later, with his newfound sobriety and a genuine spiritual awakening unfolding, David wondered if psilocybin could help him dive deeper. This time, it wouldn't be about recreation or escape. It would be intentional, sacred. He had learned that Colorado had decriminalized psilocybin mushrooms, and the therapeutic field was beginning to embrace them for mental health treatment.

He couldn't shake the feeling that this was no coincidence.

"I'm not trying to run away from anything," David told himself. "I'm trying to understand."

THE MISSION

David's mind was made up—he was going to procure some mushrooms. He wasn't interested in abusing them; he wanted to approach them with respect and reverence, like the indigenous cultures he had read about. He learned that ancient peoples saw psilocybin as a way to connect with the divine, to open the third eye, and to commune with spiritual realms.

The idea fascinated him. What might he see? What truths might be revealed?

David began asking around discreetly. He didn't want to draw too much attention—after all, this wasn't something he could just walk into a store and buy. But he knew that in a progressive place like Colorado, there were likely people growing their own or engaging in ceremonial use.

A Connection

One afternoon, while sharing a quiet smoke break in the courtyard, David mentioned his curiosity to Scott.

"You ever look into psilocybin?" David asked, careful not to seem too eager.

Scott's eyes lit up. "You're talking about mushrooms, right?"

David nodded.

"Man, let me tell you something," Scott said, leaning in conspiratorially. "I've read a ton about that stuff. Did you know the ancient's believed mushrooms were a gift from God? They called them 'the flesh of the gods.' And don't even get me started on how they might've been connected to manna in the Bible. I wouldn't be surprised if you're onto something, brother."

David chuckled, shaking his head. "You've always got a way of tying things back to scripture."

Scott laughed. "Hey, I'm serious, though. If you're gonna do it, you need to go into it with the right mindset. No distractions, no negativity —just you, God, and whatever He wants to show you."

Scott paused and then added, "I might know someone who could help you out. Let me make a call."

A Sacred Step
Forward

As David waited for Scott to make arrangements, he spent time preparing himself mentally and spiritually. He meditated, read more about the spiritual use of psilocybin, and prayed for guidance. This wasn't just an experiment for him; it was a step toward deepening his connection with the divine.

David couldn't help but feel like this was another sign. Everything in Colorado—the people he had met, the circumstances that had led him here—seemed to align perfectly, like pieces of a puzzle falling into place.

"Maybe this is what I've been looking for all along," he thought.

David's first journey with psilocybin began on a snowy morning, one of those rare days when the world seemed to hold its breath in quiet wonder. The snow had been falling steadily for two days, blanketing the earth in a pristine, untouched sheet of white. He had waited for this moment with a sense of reverence, preparing himself mentally and spiritually for the experience.

As the psilocybin began to take effect, he felt a warmth bloom within him, as if something ancient and wise had awoken in the core of his being. He stepped outside, and the world that greeted him was nothing short of magical.

An Enchanted Forest

The snow-covered ground sparkled like a field of diamonds, each crystal reflecting a kaleidoscope of colors that David had never noticed before. He could see the intricate patterns of each flake, so impossibly delicate and yet perfect, as if God Himself had carved each one with infinite care.

The trees stood tall and silent; their branches heavy with snow. Yet to David, they didn't feel lifeless. They pulsed with a quiet energy, an ancient wisdom that resonated through the air. He could swear he saw the faintest glow emanating from them, as if the snow had trapped the light of the heavens and was sharing it with the earth.

The entire scene shimmered as though it existed between worlds, a place where the divine and the mortal intertwined. The falling snow seemed to dance around him, slow and deliberate, as if the universe had choreographed this moment just for him.

TEARS OF GRATITUDE

David stood still, his breath visible in the crisp air, his heart pounding with an overwhelming sense of awe. Tears began to stream down his face —not from sadness, but from a profound, uncontainable gratitude.

He whispered softly, "Thank you, God."

In that moment, he felt as though he could hear the heartbeat of creation itself. Each flake of snow, each whisper of wind, and every creak of the trees was part of a grand, celestial symphony.

It was as if the entire universe was alive, and he was a cherished part of it. For the first time in years, he felt truly seen, as though the Creator had orchestrated this moment to remind him of the beauty, he had been blind to for so long.

VISIONS AND MESSAGES

As David walked through the snow, his senses heightened, he began to notice signs all around him. The tracks of a deer wove a graceful path through the snow, and he couldn't help but feel as though it symbolized his own journey—a reminder to tread softly and to trust the path even when it wasn't clear. Eddy's words, "Trust the process", rang in his ears. A phrase that seemed to leap at him from places since he first told him that.

At one point, he stopped and gazed up at the sky. The snowflakes fell in slow motion, each one seeming to carry a message. One flake landed on his palm, and for a fleeting moment, he felt it wasn't just a flake of snow but a piece of divine love, melting into him and becoming part of his being.

He heard no words, yet he understood. The message was simple: You are loved. You are part of something far greater than you can imagine. Keep walking.

A Glimpse of the Infinite

As David stood in the stillness, he began to feel a connection to everything around him—the trees, the snow, the earth beneath his feet. It was as though the barriers between him and the world had dissolved, and he was no longer separate.

He closed his eyes and saw vivid, kaleidoscopic patterns of light that seemed to pulse in rhythm with his breathing. Within the patterns, he saw glimpses of his past, moments of hardship and pain, and then flashes of his future—his potential, his purpose.

He saw himself standing in a room, surrounded by people, sharing his story, helping others find their way. He felt a surge of warmth in his chest, a sense of calling so powerful it brought him to his knees in the snow.

Returning to the Present

When David finally returned to his room, the snow still falling outside, he sat by the window, watching the flakes dance against the glass. He felt a deep calm, a profound sense of belonging.

He knew this was just the beginning of his journey, but for the first time, he felt ready to embrace it fully. He whispered another prayer of thanks, knowing that this moment would stay with him forever.

In the days that followed, David found himself seeing the world in a new light. The psilocybin journey had left a profound impression on him, a sense that the veil between the mundane and the divine had been lifted, if only for a moment. He felt an awareness that went beyond words, an inner peace that tempered his restless spirit.

A Shift in Perspective

Walking through the halls of the HOPE Program, David noticed details he'd previously overlooked—the way light filtered through the windows, creating patterns on the floor, the gentle hum of people talking, the kindness in their laughter. He felt as if he was viewing life through a lens of gratitude.

Even small tasks like cleaning or organizing his room felt purposeful. He started writing in a journal each night, recording not only his thoughts but the small miracles he noticed throughout the day. He began with his snow-filled experience, describing it in intricate detail, and as he wrote, he found clarity about the importance of this moment in his life.

David also spent more time in prayer, not asking for anything, but simply thanking God for the beauty in his life and the strength to keep moving forward.

Conversations with Scott

Scott, ever eager to discuss spiritual matters, noticed David's shift in demeanor.

"You look different," Scott said one evening over dinner. "Like something clicked."

David nodded. "I think it has. That snowstorm the other day—it wasn't just weather. It was like God was speaking to me through the world, showing me how connected everything is."

Scott leaned in; his eyes bright. "That's exactly it, man. Creation speaks to us all the time, but most people aren't listening. You're waking up. The chosen ones always do."

David smiled, still unsure about the term "chosen one" but finding it harder to deny. Scott's words carried a resonance now, as if pieces of a puzzle were starting to fit together.

NEW HABITS AND DISCOVERIES

Inspired by his experience, David began meditating each morning. He found a quiet corner of the building where he could sit undisturbed, focusing on his breath and the stillness around him. During one meditation, he imagined himself walking through the snow again, and as he did, he felt a warmth wash over him, as if God was reminding him of the peace he'd found.

David also started attending the optional Bible study sessions led by the program chaplain. Though he had read the Bible before, the verses now seemed to leap off the page with new meaning. One day, the chaplain read from **Isaiah 1:18**:

"Though your sins are like scarlet, they shall be as white as snow; though they are red as crimson, they shall be like wool."

The words struck David deeply, and he felt tears welling in his eyes. He thought of the snow again, its purity and beauty, and how it mirrored God's grace in his life. In the days that followed, David found himself seeing the world in a new light. The psilocybin journey had left a profound impression on him, a sense that the veil between the mundane and the divine had been lifted, if only for a moment. He felt an awareness that went beyond words, an inner peace that tempered his restless spirit.

A New Sense of Purpose

One evening, while journaling, David realized that his experience with the snow was more than just a moment of beauty—it was a calling. He began thinking about the people he could help, the lives he could touch.

Eddy's journey to Colorado, Scott's boldness, and even the random Uber driver with the shared birthday all seemed like pieces of a larger plan. He felt compelled to share his story, not just for himself but for those who might need to hear it.

FIRST STEPS TOWARD ACTION

David approached his chaplain a few days later. "I think I've been given a second chance," he said. "And I want to use it to help others."

The chaplain smiled knowingly. "You're on the right path, David. God doesn't waste a single moment of our lives, even the hard ones. Sometimes, those are the ones He uses most."

The chaplain suggested David join a mentorship group within the program, where he could share his experiences with newcomers and help them navigate their own struggles.

Though nervous, David agreed. For the first time in a long time, he felt not only that he was healing but that he had something to give back.

THE CURVEBALL

One evening, David received an unexpected text from a blond-haired girl named Sarah a woman he had briefly dated back in Corpus Christi. Her message was casual at first, asking how he'd been and if he still lived in Corpus. When David explained that he had moved to Denver and was in a recovery program, Sarah's tone shifted. She confided that she was struggling—trapped in a cycle of addiction and desperation—and asked if she could come stay with him.

At first, David felt a pang of empathy. He remembered the bond they'd shared, however fleeting, and the way she had once leaned on him during hard times.

Without hesitation, he offered to help her get into recovery, even going so far as to purchase a bus ticket for her to come to Denver.

But over the next few days, as the bus departure date loomed closer, unease began to creep into his heart. For some reason he asked her to send him a recent picture of her, she readily agreed and sent him one, when he opened the picture, he was stunned to see that she had dyed her beautiful blond hair red. Something both Jamie and Sandi did right before they started acting different towards him. Something about the situation didn't feel right. David couldn't shake the nagging thought that this wasn't just a coincidence—it was a test.

He reflected on the patterns of his past. Women had always been his weakness, a distraction that often pulled him off course. What if this wasn't just a coincidence? What if this was a spiritual attack, carefully designed to derail his progress?

Seeking Guidance

Haunted by his thoughts, David sought out the chaplain. Sitting across from her in the quiet office, he hesitated before asking, "Do you believe in the spirit of Lilith?" The story of Lilith says she was Adams original wife, created from the dust of the ground just as Adam was made by God.

The chaplain didn't flinch. "Yes, I do," she said simply. David was caught off guard by the answer. He assumed she would scoff, or laugh at the question. She continued, Lilith is the symbol of chaos, seduction, and ungodliness, and is often seen as a representation of the fallen women. Lilith is depicted with flowing red hair.

The spirit of Lilith, according to ancient lore, was said to be a powerful and malevolent force. Originating in Jewish mysticism, she was described as Adam's first wife—created as his equal but cast out of Eden for refusing to submit. Over time, she became a symbol of rebellion and seduction, a dark spiritual entity associated with luring men into sin and corrupting the innocent. Some believed she and her lesser demons preyed on the weak and vulnerable, exploiting their desires and weaknesses to lead them astray.

David exhaled, relieved by her straightforward answer. He shared his fears, explaining how he felt that Sarah's sudden reappearance was no accident. "I think one of her lesser demons is after me," he confessed, "using Sarah to pull me away from my calling."

The chaplain nodded thoughtfully. "It's possible," she said. "But remember, David: the enemy only has as much power over you as you allow. You're the one who decides whether to let that spirit back into your life."

Her words hit David like a bolt of clarity. He realized that he had the power to set boundaries, to choose the path he wanted to follow. This wasn't just about Sarah —it was about him, his strength, and his commitment to his spiritual awakening.

THE MESSAGE

That night, David sat on his bed with his journal open, pen poised above the page. He needed to find the right words to let Sarah down, to protect himself without abandoning her entirely.

Finally, he began to write:

Sarah, I've been thinking a lot about your message and what it would mean for you to come to Denver. I want to help you, and I truly care about your well-being.

But right now, I feel like this might not be the best idea—for you or for me. I'm at a point in my life where I'm deeply focused on my recovery and my spiritual growth. I'm worried that bringing you here would distract both of us from the paths we need to follow."

"I believe you have the strength to find your own way to recovery, and I'm here to support you from a distance. I'm praying for you, and I hope you can understand why I'm making this choice. Please know it comes from a place of love and care, not rejection."

As he hit "send," David felt a wave of relief wash over him. For the first time, he had chosen the harder, higher road. It wasn't about running from temptation—it was about standing firm in his purpose.

AFTERMATH

In the days that followed, David felt lighter, more focused. He noticed small signs that reassured him he had made the right choice: a random Bible verse about perseverance, a conversation with Scott that seemed to echo his inner thoughts, and a dream where he saw himself standing strong against a storm, unshaken.

Sarah responded to his message, with understanding which took David by surprise, maybe he had been wrong, but after what he went through with Jamie and Sandi, he wasn't taking any chances. His decision had been about his journey, his growth, and his unwavering commitment to God's plan.

This experience solidified David's resolve. He knew the enemy would test him again, but now he understood his power to choose—and that power, rooted in faith, was more potent than any temptation.

David's First Offsite Experience

It was an overcast Sunday when David finally earned the privilege to leave the facility and join a small group from the program on an offsite outing. The group leader, a towering man named Carl with a deep, resonant voice and a perpetual look of calm, had arranged for them to visit a nearby park known for its serene walking trails and scenic views of the Rockies.

David sat quietly in the van, watching the city blur past the window. The gray sky seemed to fit his mood—a mix of anticipation and unease. It had been over a month since he'd been outside the facility for anything other than a medical appointment. The thought of being back in the real world, even in a small way, made him feel both free and vulnerable.

When they arrived, the cool air carried a faint piney scent, and the sound of rustling leaves filled the space between the murmured conversations of the group.

David walked a few steps behind the others, taking in the surroundings. There was something almost sacred about the way the clouds hung low over the mountains, their peaks veiled in mist.

Carl encouraged everyone to split up for a while and find a quiet spot to reflect. David wandered to the edge of a small stream, where the water trickled over smooth stones. He sat down on a fallen log, his mind drifting.

As he stared into the water, a sense of peace washed over him. The natural beauty reminded him of the snowy day he had experienced during his psilocybin trip.

It was as though the universe was nudging him, whispering, remember what you saw. Don't lose sight of that clarity.

But alongside the serenity came an unsettling thought: What if this is just a brief respite, and the chaos of life will pull me back under? He tried to push the doubt away, focusing on the sound of the water and the distant chirping of birds.

When the group reconvened, Carl led them in a prayer. David bowed his head but couldn't stop his mind from wandering. He wondered if this newfound peace would last—or if it was simply a fragile illusion.

Doubts Creeping In

Back at the facility, David couldn't shake the gnawing uncertainty that had crept in at the park. While his initial weeks had been full of awe-inspiring moments and a sense of divine guidance, a part of him now began to question everything.

Sitting in his small room that evening, he flipped through his journal. The early pages were filled with passionate entries about signs and synchronicities, but as he read further, he noticed a subtle shift. Recent entries were more analytical, almost skeptical.

Was this really a spiritual awakening, or was it just my mind grasping at meaning because I'm desperate to believe in something?

He thought back to the psilocybin trip. In the moment, everything had felt so clear, so undeniably real. But now, he couldn't help but wonder if it had been nothing more than a chemically induced illusion.

The doubts became louder when he thought about Scott. David admired Scott's conviction, but he also found it overwhelming at times. Could it be that Scott's certainty was a kind of delusion? And if it was, what did that mean for David's own experiences?

That night, as he lay in bed staring at the ceiling, he whispered a prayer. "God, if You're really guiding me, please show me. Help me to know what's real and what's not. I don't want to be lost again."

It was a simple plea, spoken from a place of both faith and doubt. And as he drifted off to sleep, David felt a strange mix of unease and hope, as though he was standing on the edge of something significant—but couldn't yet see what lay ahead.

David had been working hard to maintain peace in his heart, despite the challenges around him. The rehab facility was a crucible of different personalities—some loud and opinionated, others withdrawn and distrustful, and a few whose negativity seemed to seep into the air like smoke. It wasn't easy to live in such close quarters with so many people, especially when tempers flared over petty things like who cleaned the kitchen or whose turn it was to control the remote in the common room.

But David reminded himself daily why he was here. He wasn't just fighting his old demons—he was trying to transform, to rise above the patterns that had controlled him for so long.

He'd been watching a lot of videos about Earth's supposed shift into a new reality, a 5th-dimensional state of being where love, compassion, and unity were the guiding principles. The speakers called it "New Earth," a place where humanity could transcend the limitations of fear, anger, and greed that had defined the old world.

David didn't know if all of it was true—he was still skeptical about some of the metaphysical ideas—but the concept resonated with him on a deep level. He thought about the choices he made every day: Would he let irritation and negativity pull him back into the old patterns of Old Earth, or would he choose forgiveness, kindness, and understanding, the way he imagined people would live on New Earth?

He found himself asking that question whenever a situation tested him.

Like the time someone ate his food from the fridge without asking, something that would have sent him into a rage just months ago. Instead of confronting the person angrily, he simply let it go, reasoning that they were probably hungrier than he was.

Or when one of the newer residents snapped at him for sitting in their "usual" spot in the common room. David felt his pulse quicken, the old instinct to lash out threatening to take over. But then he took a deep breath, smiled, and said, "No problem, man. It's all yours."

Every time he chose peace over anger, compassion over judgment, he felt a sense of lightness, as if he were shedding the heavy baggage of his old life. It wasn't always easy. Some days, he wanted to scream at the unfairness of it all, to remind people of everything he was sacrificing just to stay on this path. But then he remembered the videos about high vibration and alignment with the universe.

"Your frequency determines your reality," one of the speakers had said. "If you stay in fear, anger, or resentment, you'll keep yourself tethered to Old Earth. But if you choose love, gratitude, and forgiveness, you align yourself with the energy of New Earth."

David didn't want to get stuck in Old Earth. He wanted to transcend to something better, not just for himself but for the people he loved, the people he'd hurt, and even the people he hadn't met yet. He imagined what life on New Earth might be like—no more suffering, no more addiction, no more fear of the future. It was a place where everyone could live authentically, guided by love and divine purpose.

The idea filled him with hope, but it also challenged him. Could he really sustain this higher vibration, or was he just fooling himself? Was he strong enough to resist the pull of his old habits, the temptation to slip back into bitterness and despair?

The answers didn't come easily, but David decided he didn't need them right away. For now, all he could do was take each moment as it came, choosing, again and again, to rise above. To forgive. To stay in alignment.

Even if the New Earth wasn't real, he thought, wasn't it better to live as if it were? To embody the principles of love, kindness, and unity, no matter what? If nothing else, it made him feel lighter, freer, and more connected to something greater than himself.

And maybe that was the whole point.

RANTS

David often found himself captivated by Scott's stories, even if they seemed outlandish at times. Over lunch one afternoon, Scott leaned in, his voice low and conspiratorial, as if he were about to reveal one of the universe's best-kept secrets.

"Have you ever heard about the giants in the Bible?" Scott asked, his eyes gleaming with excitement.

David nodded. "You mean the Nephilim? The ones mentioned in Genesis? Yeah, I've read about them. Angels and human women, right?"

"Exactly!" Scott said, pointing at David like he'd just passed a pop quiz. "But here's the thing most people don't know—they didn't just disappear. They're still here.

Or, at least, their bloodlines are." And their spirits still roam the earth, wreaking havoc wherever they can find a foot hold.

David raised an eyebrow but stayed quiet, letting Scott continue.

"There are ancient texts, man. Stuff the church doesn't want you to know about. The giants were wiped out during the flood, sure, but not all of them. Some survived, and they're tied to what's happening now with the portals."

David leaned back, curious. "Portals?"

"Yeah, portals," Scott said, lowering his voice even further. "Stargates, wormholes, whatever you wanna call them. Think about all the weird places around the world—Skinwalker Ranch, the Bermuda Triangle, Antarctica. These places aren't just random anomalies. They're gateways to other realms. The Nephilim, or what's left of their influence, they're connected to this. And it's not just them—it's fallen angels too, still working behind the scenes to manipulate humanity. That's what the alien sightings really are. Not extraterrestrials, but interdimensional beings trying to deceive us."

what the alien sightings really are. Not extraterrestrials, but interdimensional beings trying to deceive us."

David tried to suppress a skeptical grin, but he couldn't help himself. "So you're saying these portals are like…supernatural highways?"

"Exactly!" Scott said, clearly delighted that David was at least entertaining the idea. "The governments know about it too. Why do you think they've been so hush-hush about UFOs until recently? They're prepping us for something. They'll tell us aliens are here to help, but it's all a lie. It's the fallen angels, man, coming back to finish what they started in Genesis. That's why we need to wake people up."

David wasn't entirely convinced, but there was something oddly compelling about Scott's conviction. He thought back to his own spiritual awakening, the strange signs and experiences he'd had. If those were real, who was to say Scott's theories weren't?

"You think the giants, or their descendants, are still influencing things today?" David asked.

Scott nodded emphatically. "Absolutely. Look at the ruins—Puma Punku, Baalbek, the pyramids. You think humans moved those stones? No way. The giants, their knowledge—it's all tied to those ancient sites. And those sites, they're aligned with the portals."

David thought about it for a moment. "So, what's the endgame, then? Why all the secrecy? What are these beings trying to do?"

"They want to enslave us," Scott said, his voice grave. "The fallen angels hate us because we're God's creation. They've been working against us since the beginning, corrupting humanity, leading us astray. And now, as we get closer to the end times, they're ramping up their efforts. But here's the good news—we've got the power of God on our side. If we stay strong, if we stay in alignment, they can't win."

David admired Scott's passion, even if he wasn't sure he believed everything. But the conversation stuck with him. He found himself wondering: what if there was some truth to it? What if the strange happenings in the world weren't just coincidence?

And what if, just maybe, Scott was right—there were forces at work far greater than anyone realized, pulling the strings of humanity from realms unseen?

David noticed the new guy almost immediately when he walked into the program. He had a wiry frame, a mop of unkempt brown hair, and a nose that seemed a little too big for his small face. He was short, maybe 5'4", and couldn't have weighed more than 120 pounds soaking wet. At first glance, David thought he was a teenager, but when they introduced themselves, he was shocked to learn the guy was actually 40 years old.

A New Ally

The kid—well, man—introduced himself as Jason. From the moment Jason started talking, it was clear there was something different about him. His words tumbled out at breakneck speed, jumping from topic to topic so quickly it was hard to keep up. One moment, he was talking about quantum physics; the next, he was asking if anyone had seen his favorite pen.

David tried to guide Jason where he could, recognizing his good heart and genuine nature beneath the hyperactivity. Jason's energy was boundless—he couldn't sit still, constantly tapping his foot, fiddling with objects, or wandering off mid-conversation. His ADHD was evident, and David suspected he might have a few other challenges going on upstairs.

Despite the distractions, David found himself drawn to Jason. There was something endearing about his innocence, his unfiltered enthusiasm for life, and his desire to connect with others, even if he didn't always know how to do it appropriately.

One day, Jason approached David while they were sitting outside.

"Hey, David," he began, practically vibrating with excitement. "Do you think people like us get put here for a reason?"

David raised an eyebrow. "What do you mean, 'people like us?'"

"You know," Jason said, gesturing vaguely. "People who've been through stuff. Like, maybe we're meant to help other people or something. Like...chosen."

David was taken aback. It wasn't the first time he'd heard someone mention being chosen lately, but hearing it from Jason felt different.

"Why do you say that?" David asked carefully.

Jason shrugged, his face earnest. "I don't know. I just feel like I'm supposed to be here, you know? Like, all the stuff that's wrong with me...maybe it's not wrong at all. Maybe it's just how I'm meant to be, so I can do whatever it is I'm supposed to do."

David studied him for a moment. Despite Jason's scattered mind and childlike demeanor, there was a depth to his words that surprised him. It made David wonder if Jason was right—if maybe, just maybe, he was one of the chosen ones too.

But guiding Jason wasn't easy. David tried to offer advice and steer him in the right direction, but Jason's attention span was so short that half the time, he'd already moved on to another subject before David could finish a sentence.

"Jason, focus," David said one day, exasperated after trying to explain the importance of setting boundaries with others.

"I am focusing!" Jason insisted, though he was simultaneously trying to catch a fly with his hand.

David sighed, but he couldn't help but smile. Jason might have been a challenge, but there was something pure and uncorrupted about him that David admired.

As the days went on, David started to believe that Jason's chaotic energy might not just be a quirk but a gift in disguise. It was hard to say for sure, but David had learned enough not to dismiss the possibility. God worked in mysterious ways, after all. And sometimes, the people who seemed the most unlikely were the ones chosen to make the biggest impact.

Divine Suspicions

David had suspected for a while now that Eddy might be a chosen one. There was something about the way Eddy carried himself—his relentless drive to help others, even when it was clearly taking a toll on him. As a case manager, Eddy had 13 clients under his care, each one with their own set of struggles. Many were addicts, and some had significant mental health issues.

But not everyone wanted to be helped. David could see the frustration in Eddy's eyes when he talked about the clients who were just going through the motions for the benefits. They weren't really committed to recovery, just using the program for housing or to stay out of trouble.

"It's like I'm pouring myself into an empty cup," Eddy had vented one afternoon, pacing the smoking area. "I give and I give, but they don't even want to change.

They just want to take."

David nodded, understanding. "You can't save everyone, Eddy. Sometimes people aren't ready to be saved."

"I know," Eddy said, exhaling a cloud of smoke. "But it's hard, man. I got into this to make a difference, but half the time, I feel like I'm just enabling them."

On some days, it got to be too much for Eddy. He'd call David up, asking if he wanted to get out of the building for a while. "Let's play hooky," he'd say with a mischievous grin.

They'd escape the grind for a few hours, heading to the movie theater to catch whatever was playing. David appreciated those moments with Eddy. It was a chance for both of them to recharge, to leave behind the heavy weight of the program and just be two friends sharing a laugh over a bucket of popcorn.

Still, Eddy's struggles stayed with David. He could see how much Eddy cared, how deeply he wanted to help people, even at the expense of his own peace of mind. And it made David wonder if that selflessness, that drive to serve despite the odds, was what made Eddy one of the chosen ones.

"I don't know how you do it, man," David said once after the movie.

Eddy shrugged, staring out the window of his car as they sat in the parking lot. "I don't know either. Some days, I just want to pack up and leave. Go somewhere quiet, where I don't have to deal with any of this."

"But you don't," David pointed out.

Eddy smiled faintly. "No. I don't. Because I know it's what I'm supposed to do. Even when it sucks."

David nodded, feeling a pang of admiration for his friend. Eddy might not have called himself chosen, but his actions spoke louder than any label ever could.

David thought back to the script line from the movie, "Red One" they had just watched. Dwayne "The Rock" Johnson plays Santa's personal bodyguard. He was telling his costar that we have to look at every decision as an opportunity. An opportunity to choose between doing what is right, or doing what is wrong. David found that simple truth profound.

One With Humanity

Over the next week, David noticed a shift in himself—subtle but profound. He began to feel a wellspring of love and compassion for people he barely knew. It was as if the boundaries between him and the world around him had blurred, and he could sense the weight others carried.

One afternoon, while sitting outside in the smoke pit of the NLRM, David decided to take a small dose of psilocybin mushrooms on his own. He wasn't looking for a trip, just a deeper connection with the world and his thoughts. As the mushrooms took hold, the familiar surroundings of the smoke pit transformed into a living mosaic.

He sat quietly, blending into the scene, listening to the buzz of conversations around him. The space was alive with the rawness of humanity: a young man confided in a friend about his struggles with addiction, a group of women laughed over shared stories, and a solitary figure sat in the corner, staring off into the distance.

David's gaze moved from face to face, his heart aching as he absorbed the myriad emotions playing out before him. There were people who exuded joy, their laughter like sunlight cutting through the grayness. Others wore their pain visibly, their eyes clouded with bitterness, confusion, or despair. It was a tapestry of life, woven with threads of hope and suffering.

As he sat there, a deep sadness began to creep into his chest. He thought about all the people he'd loved and lost over the years—the family members who had passed, the friends who had faded away, the women who had left him brokenhearted. Memories of his time in prison resurfaced, the isolation, the anger, and the emptiness that had consumed him.

Unable to sit with the overwhelming wave of emotion, David quietly made his way inside, retreating to the solitude of his bathroom. The walls seemed to close in as he sank to the floor, his head in his hands. Tears began to flow, slowly at first, but then uncontrollably, as if a dam had burst.

He cried for all the pain humanity endured, for the struggles etched into every face he had seen outside. He cried for himself—for the years of suffering, the mistakes, the moments when he felt abandoned and forgotten. Every loss, every betrayal, every wound he thought he had buried came rushing to the surface.

The sobs racked his body, raw and unrelenting. It felt like hours passed, though time seemed meaningless in that moment. He cried until he could cry no more, his body drained, his heart hollowed out.

When the tears finally stopped, David sat in silence, his breathing shallow and uneven. There was an odd stillness within him, as though he had shed a layer of himself, leaving something raw and vulnerable behind.

Looking at his reflection in the mirror, his eyes swollen and red, he whispered, "God, I don't know why you've kept me here. But if there's a reason, show me the way. I'm tired of carrying this alone."

In that moment, David felt a faint flicker of hope, like the smallest ember in a vast darkness. It wasn't much, but it was enough to hold onto.

THE TRANSFORMATION

One afternoon, David stumbled upon an inspirational video that captured his attention. It told the story of the bald eagle, a majestic bird renowned for its strength and grace. But there was a lesser-known chapter in the eagle's life—a period of profound struggle and transformation.

When an eagle reaches a certain age, its once-sharp beak and talons become too dull to hunt effectively, and its feathers grow ragged, weighing it down and making flight a laborious task. At this crossroads, the eagle has two choices: give up and die, or endure a grueling renewal process.

The video explained how, if the eagle chooses to live, it flies to the mountains, far from distractions and danger. There, it begins the painful transformation. First, the eagle bashes its beak against the rocks until the old, worn beak falls off. In time, a new, sharp beak grows in its place. Then, using its renewed beak, the eagle plucks out its own talons, one by one. Fresh, razor-sharp talons grow back in their stead. Finally, the eagle meticulously removes its old feathers, each one torn away to make room for new, sleek plumage. This arduous process takes about 180 days, but when it is complete, the eagle emerges reborn—strong, renewed, and ready to soar once more.

As David watched, he couldn't help but draw parallels to his own life. He had ridden' up from Texas to Colorado, leaving behind the remnants of his old, worn-out existence. Here, in the shadow of the Rockies, he had entered a program that also spanned roughly 180 days before he was allowed to actually go out and start looking for a job—the same length of time it took the eagle to transform.

The connection felt too meaningful to ignore. David reflected on the symbolic message: like the eagle, he had reached a breaking point in his life. His old tools — his habits, his way of thinking, his approach to life—were no longer serving him. If he wanted to survive, he couldn't rely on who he used to be. He would have to endure the pain of breaking down the old parts of himself, stripping away the layers of anger, fear, and self-doubt, so that he could grow into the man he was meant to become.

Sitting there, David felt an overwhelming sense of reassurance. This was no coincidence; it was a message from God and the universe. He realized that he was exactly where he was supposed to be. The challenges he faced were not punishments but opportunities for transformation. The mountains, the timeline, even the difficult moments he endured in the program—they were all part of a divine plan.

"This is my time," David thought. "I'm not here to give up. I'm here to grow."

With a renewed sense of purpose, David resolved to embrace the process, no matter how difficult it might be. Just like the eagle, he was preparing to soar again, stronger than ever before.

Temptation's Heart

Out of the blue, after two months of silence, my phone lit up with a text from Sandi. Her name on the screen sent a ripple of emotions through me—confusion, concern, and, if I were honest with myself, a flicker of something softer. I opened the message, and her words tumbled out in a mix of regret and desperation.

"Where are you?" she asked.

I told her the truth: "I'm in Denver now, working on myself, trying to get right."

Her response took me off guard. She didn't press me for details or berate me for leaving her behind; instead, she opened up about her struggles. She said she'd been living on the streets, stealing food just to survive, and was sure she'd be caught and end up in jail soon.

"Why don't you go back home to your mom in Fort Worth?" I asked, hoping she had some kind of lifeline.

Her answer was bleak: "She can't even send me five dollars to eat, let alone help me get there."

As much as I tried to keep my heart guarded, it cracked a little. Sandi had been a tornado in my life—destructive and chaotic—but she was still human, still someone I'd cared about. I asked her about Gee Bee, my dog, and she claimed she'd seen her. "Yeah, she's okay," she said. But her words felt distant, like she wasn't telling the whole truth.

Then she said something that tugged at me: "I was stupid not to go with you to Denver. Things might've been different."

I couldn't argue with her. Deep down, I knew that if we'd made the move together, some of the disasters we'd lived through might have been avoided. But life doesn't offer do-overs.

I couldn't let her starve. "Can you get to the store tomorrow?" I asked. "I'll order you $20 worth of food online, and you can pick it up."

She agreed, and I followed through. I didn't do it because I wanted anything from her, or because I still had feelings for her, besides as a person and a child of God. I did it because no one deserves to go hungry. Whatever wrongs she'd done, she was still a person in need, and I'd forgiven her. Forgiveness didn't mean I could ever trust her again or let her back into my life—it simply meant I was letting go of the bitterness.

Over the next couple of days, she sent a few more texts. I found myself in a strange emotional limbo—part of me felt like I was being tested. This was Sandi, after all. A woman who had manipulated, lied, and left me broken more times than I could count. But I also saw her as a mirror of the past, a reminder of the person I'd been—the choices I'd made, the pain I'd caused myself and others.

When she mentioned again how much she wanted to go to Fort Worth, I considered buying her a bus ticket. I even told her I'd try to scrape the money together.

But when I texted her later to say I couldn't do it right now, the line went silent. No reply.

It stung more than I wanted to admit. Was she expecting me to jump through hoops for her? To rescue her again, like I had so many times before? Or was this her way of closing the door, realizing I wasn't going to be the person I used to be?

I told myself I had done what I could. The old David might have bent over backward, trying to win her approval or fix her problems, but I wasn't that man anymore. I had worked too hard to find a shred of peace in my life, to break free from the cycle of enabling and being taken advantage of.

Still, the whole situation left me questioning—was this a genuine cry for help, or just another trick of the enemy, trying to drag me back into old patterns?

Temptations come in many forms, and sometimes they wear familiar faces. This one had Lilith's name written all over it. At one time Sandi had spoken to me in the third person, claiming to be Lilith, stating that Sandi was weak. And that from then on, she would be running the show, because Sandi couldn't be trusted, that she was foolish for believing in love.

Lilith's Shadow

The last message I got from Sandi left me unsettled, but it wasn't until I put my phone down that the weight of everything hit me. This wasn't just Sandi reaching out; it felt like something else—something darker. I'd seen this before. That creeping shadow, that manipulative edge disguised as need and despair. This had Lilith's name written all over it. David wasn't about to let that spirit manipulate him any longer, his walk with Christ had become a major turning point in his life—he was done with that old life, or so he thought at the time.

Flashback: The Black Pyramid

It was supposed to be a good night, an escape. Jamie and I had been through so much already, and when we got our hands on some Black Pyramid LSD, we thought it'd be a way to reconnect, to tap into something beyond the struggles of our everyday lives. But we had no idea what we were playing with.

The trip hit Jamie harder than it hit me. I noticed it within the first hour—her breathing changed, and her eyes darted around the room as if she were seeing something none of us could. At first, she just seemed scared, mumbling things about her childhood, about her dad. But then the fear turned into something else.

She was crying, clutching her head, and muttering," No, no, I can't go back there."

I tried to calm her down, but it was as if the barriers in her mind had crumbled, leaving her defenseless. That's when the screaming started— not just cries of fear, but guttural, otherworldly screams that chilled me to the bone.

I didn't know it at the time, but I was witnessing the moment her soul cracked open just wide enough for something else to slip inside. Something ancient and malevolent.

The Change

After that night, Jamie dyed her hair red—a shade so bright it was almost unnatural. At first I thought it was just her way of coping, a way of reclaiming control after what shed gone through. But the change wasn't just physical.

She started walking differently, talking differently. She started withholding sex from me, and when we did make love, she always wanted to be on top. Her voice carried an edge, her words laced with bitterness and venom. She began fixating on ideas of fairness and equality, twisting them into accusations.

"You're selfish," she'd say, her tone sharp and unfamiliar. "You always get more than I do. You always do what you want." It's not fair!

This wasn't the Jamie I knew. It was like living with a stranger who wore her face.

One day, during a particularly bad argument, I stormed off, or at least I pretended to. I wanted space, but curiosity got the better of me, so I made fake footsteps, making it sound like I was leaving the room. Then I stood outside the doorway, listening. That's when I heard it.

Two Voices

The first was Jamie's, trembling and pleading, "Oh no, it's happening again."

The second was something I'll never forget. Raspy, guttural, and almost mocking, it replied, "But he's done more for you than all the others have."

A chill ran down my spine. There was no one else in the room. My heart raced as I jumped back into the doorway. "Who the hell were you talking to?" I demanded.

Jamie froze, her face pale. "What are you talking about? I was just talking to myself," she said, her voice steady but her eyes darting everywhere but at me.

"No, you weren't," I shot back. "That wasn't just you. I heard someone else!"

She shrugged, trying to play it off. "I talk to myself in the third person sometimes."

"No," I insisted, my voice rising. "That wasn't third-person anything. It sounded like someone else was in here!"

Her gaze finally met mine, but there was something guarded behind it. "You're tripping," she muttered, turning away.

But I wasn't. I'd heard it. I knew what I'd heard.

THE POSSESSION

Over the next few weeks, things only got worse. Jamie became secretive, sneaky, as if she were constantly scheming. One night, she asked me for something that sent alarm bells ringing: a drop of my blood.

"Just one drop," she said, her voice almost pleading.

"What? Why the hell would you need my blood?"

"It's for protection," she claimed, her words quick and desperate.

When I refused, her expression darkened. Her face twisted in a way I can only describe as inhuman—her eyes seemed to blacken, and her features contorted into something sinister.

"There it is," I whispered, stepping back in horror. "I see it now."

For a moment, she seemed to snap out of it, her face clearing as she looked at me with wide, innocent eyes. "What are you talking about?" she asked, her voice trembling.

But I knew what I'd seen. I'd been feeling it for weeks—that she wasn't alone inside herself. I even confided in a couple of friends, telling them I thought she was possessed. One of them suggested I see a curandera, a healer who might be able to shed some light on the situation.

I sought out a curandera, which didn't take me long in Corpus Christi, TX. Her reading was chilling. She told me, "There are two women in your life. One is filled with love and family. The other is angry, vengeful, and wants to destroy you."

I knew immediately which one was which.

The Breaking Point

I confronted Jamie one last time. "I know what's happening," I told her. "I know you're not yourself. There's something inside you."

She laughed, a cold, hollow sound that didn't belong to her. "You're crazy," she said.

But I wasn't. I could feel it—the darkness that had taken hold of her, lurking just beneath the surface.

Soon after, everything unraveled. I started finding explicit pictures on her phone, evidence of her sneaking around with other men. She'd disappear for days, returning with half-hearted excuses. I wanted to save her, but I didn't know how. I found her journals filled with scrawled pages and pages with only four words over and over: Jaime the black-hearted.

One night, I called her out on everything. "You're not the Jamie I fell in love with. Something's wrong with you, and you won't even admit it."

Her response was venomous. "You're the problem, David. You've always been the problem."

That was the moment I realized there was no saving her. Whatever had taken hold of Jamie wasn't going to let go. And no matter how much I loved her; I couldn't let it drag me down too.

From that point on, I started distancing myself, though the damage was already done. Jamie's life spiraled further out of control, and I was left haunted by the memory of the woman I once loved—the woman who, for a brief time, was the light of my life before the darkness took her.

And as I looked back on it all, I couldn't shake the feeling that the demon hadn't just taken her. It was still out there, watching me, waiting for its next chance.

After everything I'd been through with Jamie, I thought I'd seen it all. But Sandi... Sandi was different. Or at least, I thought she was.

When we first got together, there was a light about her—something warm, inviting. She felt like my second chance, like maybe I could finally get it right. But looking back now, I see the warning signs were there from the start.

It wasn't until after she started smoking K2 that everything began to change. I believe that was the crack in her armor, the drug that broke down the walls of her mind and let something darker slip in. Something ancient. Something malevolent. Something... familiar.

A Familiar Darkness

Sandi and Jamie had been close once, back when I was in jail. At the time, I didn't think much of it. It made sense—they were both in the same circle, leaning on each other while I was gone. But after Sandi dyed her hair red, it was like she wasn't even the same person anymore.

She started doing and saying things that reminded me of Jamie— things that sent chills down my spine. At first, I chalked it up to coincidence. Then I thought maybe it was some sick game, some twisted plan the two of them had cooked up to mess with me. Maybe Jamie had sent Sandi after me to wreck my life, to make sure I never found peace.

But now, I don't think that's what happened.

I think what happened to Jamie happened to Sandi, too.

The Change

Sandi became sneaky, secretive. She was always glued to her phone, hiding whatever she was doing. One day, when she was asleep, I decided to find out for myself.

I went through her phone and what I found confirmed my worst fears. Messages to other guys, talking about explicit sex. Conversations with her friends, criticizing me, saying she was tired of listening to me "complain all the time." Sayin hurtful things that begin to gnaw away at my love for her. The more I replayed the messages in my mind the more furious I became. The betrayal cut him bone deep.

That hurt. But what struck me the most was the language she started using. She began to sound just like Jamie.

She started talking about "equality" and "fairness," about how I was always the one getting what I wanted, how I was the selfish one, how everything was my fault.

It was like she'd taken a page right out of Jamie's playbook, as if the words weren't even her own but something planted in her mind.

That's when she got ugly. Real ugly.

Her once warm and loving demeanor was replaced by bitterness and anger. She'd snap at me over the smallest things, talk down to me, call me names. The love that had once been there was gone, replaced by this venom that seemed to come from nowhere.

THE PATTERN

The more I thought about it, the more I started to see the pattern. The red hair. The sudden personality shift. The same words, the same behaviors. It wasn't just Sandi. This had Lilith's name written all over it.

I believe that whatever had taken hold of Jamie had found its way into Sandi. Maybe it was because they were close once, or maybe it was just waiting for the right moment, the right weakness to exploit.

But this time, I saw it coming. I knew the signs.

The Breaking Point

Sandi and I started fighting more and more. She'd accuse me of being the problem, of being selfish, of always putting myself first. She twisted everything around, made me question myself, my sanity.

I tried to reason with her, to get through to her, but it was no use. The Sandi I'd fallen for was gone, replaced by something cold and cruel.

One day, after a particularly bad argument, I looked her in the eyes and said, "This isn't you. I don't know what's inside you, but I know it's not you."

She just laughed, a hollow, joyless sound that sent a shiver down my spine. "Maybe this is who I've always been," she said, her voice dripping with venom.

But I didn't believe that. Not for a second.

Aftermath

I stayed for longer than I should have, hoping that somehow, I could save her, that I could bring her back. But the truth is, once Lilith gets her claws into someone, it's almost impossible to pull them out.

In the end, I had to walk away.

But even now, I can't shake the feeling that Lilith isn't done with me. She's already taken two women I cared about, twisted them, turned them against me. And I can't help but wonder... who's next?

One thing is for sure: this fight isn't over. Not by a long shot.

That question haunted me more than anything: Why me? Why was Lilith so fixated on tearing my life apart? What could I possibly have done to warrant her relentless pursuit?

I'm no saint—far from it. I've made my share of mistakes, hurt people, let my own desires and selfishness lead me astray more times than I can count. But none of that seemed enough to warrant this. This wasn't just bad luck or karma catching up with me. It was personal.

I thought back to everything I'd ever heard about Lilith. She's the embodiment of rebellion, the one who refused to submit, cast out of Eden because she wouldn't bow to Adam. She's been called a demon, a seductress, a symbol of unyielding independence and rage. But why would someone like her care about someone bow to Adam. She's been called a demon, a seductress, a symbol of unyielding independence and rage. But why would someone like her care about someone like me?

Searching for
Answers

The more I thought about it, the more I realized this went deeper than anything I could see on the surface. It wasn't just about Jamie or Sandi or even the pain she had caused me directly. It felt ancient, like a thread connecting me to something bigger than myself, something I didn't fully understand.

Maybe it had to do with the calling I'd felt my entire life—the feeling that God had a plan for me, even when I couldn't see it. A plan that I resisted, ran from, and ignored for years. What if that calling wasn't just about me? What if it was about standing in the way of something bigger?

What if Lilith saw me not as who I was, but as who I was meant to become?

Her Motive

If there's one thing I know about her, it's that she thrives on destruction. She feeds on chaos, thrives on breaking people down, especially those with the potential to rise up and challenge her influence. Maybe that's why she's after me—because I've been weak, because I've fallen into her traps before. Maybe she thinks if she can break me completely, I'll never be strong enough to fulfill my purpose.

Or maybe it's revenge. Maybe in some way I can't comprehend, I've already crossed her, already become a threat without even knowing it. Perhaps every time I've picked myself up, every time I've found the strength to move forward, it's been a slap in her face.

A Spiritual War

What if this wasn't just about me? What if it was about the bigger picture—a spiritual war where I'm just a pawn, but one she desperately wants to knock off the board?

The Bible says our battle isn't against flesh and blood, but against spiritual forces of evil in the heavenly realms. I've always believed that. I've seen too much not to. And maybe that's why Lilith is so determined to keep me down.

Because the closer I get to God, the harder it becomes for her to win.

The "why" may never fully make sense to me. Maybe I'll never know what I did to draw her wrath, or if I even did anything at all.

But one thing is clear: whatever her reason, she's determined to stop me. And if she's fighting this hard to take me down, maybe it's because there's something in me worth fighting for. Something only my walk with God will reveal.

I just hope I can figure it out before it's too late.

Reckoning with the Past

The streets of Denver were quiet in the early morning, the kind of silence that felt sacred. David shuffled along, hands deep in his jacket pockets, his breath forming faint clouds in the crisp air. He wasn't sure where he was going, just walking to clear his head.

Then he heard it.

The soft, mournful strains of a violin echoed down the street. He stopped mid-step, his ears straining to catch the melody. It was hauntingly familiar, though he couldn't place it. Following the sound, he turned the corner and saw a man sitting on a battered stool, his violin case open at his feet. The man was older, his face weathered, his fingers nimble as they coaxed life from the strings.

David froze, the music tugging at something deep inside him.

Suddenly, he was no longer in Denver.

The Flashback

He was ten years old again, sitting on a curb outside the dingy motel where his mother had left him. It was dark, and the streetlights flickered as if they might give out any second. His stomach growled, but the hunger wasn't the worst of it. The worst was the emptiness. The bone-deep loneliness.

He hugged his knees to his chest, trying to block out the sounds of arguing coming from one of the rooms nearby. Tears stung his eyes, but he refused to let them fall. Crying won't bring her back.

"A boy like you shouldn't be out here alone."

The voice startled him. He looked up to see a woman standing a few feet away. She was tall, with a presence that felt both gentle and commanding. Her hair shimmered under the streetlights, and her eyes seemed to see right through him, with such a blue as he'd never seen before.

"I'm fine," David mumbled, wiping his nose on his sleeve.

She crouched down; her gaze steady. "No, you're not. But you will be." David didn't know what to say. People didn't talk to him like that —like he mattered.

"Why are you here?" he asked finally, his voice small.

The woman smiled, a sad, knowing smile. "To remind you that

you're never truly alone. You have a purpose, even if you don't see it yet."

David frowned. "What purpose?"

"You'll know when it's time."

She reached into her coat pocket and pulled out a small, battered book. She held it out to him.

"What's this?" he asked, taking it hesitantly.

"Words to hold onto when the darkness feels too heavy."

Before David could ask her name, she stood and walked away, disappearing into the night.

When he opened the book, he saw it was a Bible. He didn't understand much of it back then, but the words stayed with him. They carried him through the years, even when he thought he'd forgotten them.

Back in the Present

The violin's last note hung in the air, pulling David back to the Denver Street. He stood there, blinking, his heart pounding.

Had that woman been real? Or had she been something else entirely?

He approached the musician, dropping a few crumpled bills into the open violin case. The man looked up, nodding in thanks, and for a split second, David thought he saw the same eyes as the woman from his memory.

The man said nothing, just smiled and returned to his playing.

As David walked away, the melody lingered in his mind, stirring something deep within him—a faint glimmer of hope, like the first light of dawn breaking through the darkness.

RECKONING WITH THE PAST (CONTINUED)

As David walked, the violin's haunting melody became a tether, drawing his thoughts deeper into a chasm of memories. The past pressed against him, vivid and unrelenting. Each step seemed heavier than the last, as though unseen chains had fastened themselves to his ankles.

Denver's streets, usually bustling, now felt deserted and surreal. Shadows stretched unnaturally, warping his surroundings into something alien. He paused in a quiet alley, the faint hum of streetlights above doing little to stave off the sensation of being watched.

He leaned against the cold brick wall and exhaled shakily. His breath clouded in the night air, but it wasn't the chill causing him to tremble. The woman's face from his memory burned in his mind. The words she spoke, the verses she recited, echoed louder than the noises around him.

"You've been marked," her voice seemed to whisper again. "You carry something they fear."

David ran a hand through his hair and muttered to himself, "Why now? Why me? What did I do to deserve this?" His own voice sounded hollow, unconvincing.

The alley fell silent, save for the faint murmur of the city beyond. He turned abruptly, feeling as if someone—or something—had called his name. But no one was there.

THE SHELTER

He wandered aimlessly until his feet led him to a church. Its tall spire seemed to pierce the night sky, and a warm light spilled from the open doors. Above the entrance hung a simple banner: "All who are weary, come and rest."

Aaron hesitated on the steps, his hand lingering on the cold metal railing. He stared at the door, his pulse quickening. It felt like stepping into a courtroom, one where every mistake, failure, and regret would be laid bare.

But the pull was undeniable. Taking a deep breath, he crossed the threshold.

The sanctuary was quiet, save for the faint rustling of someone lighting candles near the altar. The flickering flames cast long shadows, dancing across the walls like restless spirits. Aaron took a seat in the back, keeping his head low, as though trying to go unnoticed.

The weight of the room pressed on him, heavy yet oddly comforting. His eyes wandered to the cross above the altar, its silhouette stark against the backdrop of stained glass. He stared at it for what felt like hours, thoughts churning like a storm within him.

An Unexpected Conversation

A soft voice broke through his reverie. "You look troubled."

David flinched slightly and turned to see a man seated a few rows away. He was older, with a kind face etched with lines of experience. His clothes were simple, his demeanor unassuming.

David hesitated, then shrugged. "Yeah. You could say that."

The man nodded, as if he understood more than David had said. "Sometimes, the hardest battles are the ones we fight within ourselves."

David leaned back, the words striking a nerve. "What if the battle isn't just inside? What if...what if something's after me?"

The man tilted his head slightly. "You mean someone? Or something else?"

David hesitated. He didn't want to sound insane, but the words spilled out anyway. He spoke of the voices, the transformations in Jamie and Sandi, the eerie similarities between them. The red hair, the whispers of equality and fairness, the inexplicable feeling that a shadow had been following him for years.

By the time he finished, he realized his hands were trembling.

The man didn't flinch. Instead, he leaned forward, his gaze steady. "You've described what many would dismiss as coincidence. But I've seen enough to know better. What you're dealing with isn't just bad luck. It's a battle for your soul."

David blinked, his throat tightening. "Why me? I'm no one. Just some guy who's screwed up more times than I can count."

The man's expression softened. "That's exactly why. Evil doesn't waste its time on the indifferent. It targets those who have the potential to make a difference."

The words hung in the air, unsettling yet strangely affirming.

David laughed bitterly. "And what am I supposed to do about it? Fight demons? I can't even fight my own screw-ups."

The man smiled faintly. "You start by deciding who you want to be. Evil preys on the aimless, the lost. But once you know your purpose, you'll have the strength to resist."

A Glimmer of Resolve

Later that night, David sat alone in the quiet sanctuary. The flickering candles seemed to whisper secrets, their glow reflecting off the stained glass in fragmented patterns.

He didn't know how to pray, not really. But he felt compelled to speak, if only to break the silence.

"God," he said quietly, his voice thick with uncertainty. "I don't even know if You're listening. I'm not sure I'd listen to me, either."

He paused, staring at his hands. "But if You are...I need to understand. Why this is happening. Why me. And what I'm supposed to do."

The room didn't answer. But something shifted—a sensation, faint but undeniable, like the first rays of sunlight breaking through storm clouds.

For the first time in what felt like forever, David didn't feel entirely alone.

He rose to his feet; his legs unsteady but determined. He didn't have all the answers, not yet. But he had the faintest sense of direction, a whisper of clarity. And for now, that was enough to take the next step.

Unique Perspective

In the 2024 presidential race, the primary candidates were Joe Biden (Democratic Party), Donald Trump (Republican Party), and Kamala Harris, who has taken a unique position by running as an Independent after diverging from traditional party strategies. The campaign has been fraught with tension, including assassination attempts against Trump, highlighting the high stakes and division within the country. These attacks reflect not only the dangers of the political climate but also the growing sense of unrest nationwide.

David, living through Denver's bitter winter, watches the unfolding race with an unusual interest. Though he has never considered himself political, nor cast a vote even when eligible, he finds himself wanting Trump to win. David can't pinpoint the reason for this sudden preference—perhaps it's Trump's brazen defiance of the establishment or his focus on individualism that aligns with David's life philosophy. It feels like an instinctive pull, a connection to the narrative of fighting against odds.

As David reflects on this, he notices a parallel between the heated political battles and his own struggles. Just as Trump remains undeterred despite attempts on his life, David sees his journey mirrored in the resilience of the campaign. The bitter winds of Denver and the contentious race seem to amplify the inner resolve David feels growing within him—one shaped by hardship, reflection, and the hope for a better future.

FOCUSED

---David's days at the New Life Rescue Mission started to find a rhythm. As someone who had been through the intake process himself, he was assigned to assist new arrivals. It was a role that required patience and empathy, as many of the newcomers arrived with the same haunted eyes and weary resignation David had worn not long ago. Some were young men who had fallen into addiction or lost their jobs; others were older, their faces weathered from decades of struggle.

David helped them fill out paperwork, gave them a brief tour of the facility, and talked them through the rules and expectations. He noticed how much of a difference a kind word or a steady presence could make. It wasn't much, but for someone walking into a shelter for the first time, it could mean the world.

He also began taking on additional responsibilities, like helping to distribute meals in the cafeteria and volunteering to clean the dormitories. These tasks were more than a routine for David—they gave him a sense of purpose, a break from the endless loop of self-doubt and regret that used to define his days. It wasn't redemption, but it was a step in the right direction.

One afternoon during Bible study, the group sat in a circle in the mission's dimly lit chapel, discussing passages from Ephesians about spiritual warfare. David found himself deeply engaged, more so than he expected. The facilitator, a middle-aged man named Pastor Greg, had a knack for bringing scripture to life, connecting it to the struggles many in the room faced.

Midway through the session, someone brought up an article they'd read about the Church of Satan being allowed to sponsor after-school programs in public schools. A murmur of disbelief and disapproval rippled through the group. David felt a visceral reaction—part disgust, part confusion.

"Wait, you're telling me they're letting kids be exposed to that kind of thing, in a school?" he said, his voice rising.

Pastor Greg nodded solemnly. "It's a free country," he said, "but freedom of religion cuts both ways. They've argued it's about equality, that if Christians can have programs, they should too."

David shook his head, struggling to process it. "What's the world coming to? It's like... it's like evil isn't even hiding anymore. It's just out in the open."

The group fell silent, the weight of David's words settling over them. Pastor Greg spoke softly. "The Bible warns us about this, David. In the last days, there will be people who call evil good and good evil. Our job is to be the light in the darkness, no matter how dark it gets."

PRESENCE

That night, David's sleep was restless. His dreams were a chaotic swirl of faces, shadows, and whispers. He woke up drenched in sweat, his heart racing. As he sat on his bunk, trying to calm himself, he felt a strange presence in the room—an oppressive weight, as though something unseen was watching him.

For a moment, he thought he was imagining it, but then his breath turned visible in the cold air, despite the heater humming faintly nearby. His Bible lay on the nightstand, and without thinking, he reached for it, gripping it tightly as if it were a shield. The heaviness lifted almost immediately, leaving David shaken but unharmed.

The next morning, he recounted the experience to Pastor Greg, who listened intently. "David, spiritual warfare is real. Sometimes it's subtle, but other times it manifests physically, especially when you're walking closer to God. You're a threat to the enemy now, and he knows it."

The conversation left David with more questions than answers, but it also strengthened his resolve. He began to pray more fervently and to take the teachings at the mission to heart.

An Unexpected Visitor

---The night Daniel arrived at the New Life Rescue Mission; a quiet sense of purpose emanated from him. Though he appeared like any other man seeking shelter —a little disheveled, wearing a weathered coat, and carrying a small bag—there was something about him that seemed... otherworldly. The staff welcomed him, going through the usual intake process, but he offered no more than the necessary details: his name, Daniel, and that he'd come from "far away."

From the moment he walked through the doors, unseen forces stirred. The air in the mission seemed lighter, almost charged, though no one but Daniel noticed.

DANIEL

In the celestial realms long before, Daniel had stood among the angels, fulfilling his duties with reverence. But a single moment of defiance—born not out of malice, but out of a deep love for humanity—had set him apart. While his brethren followed God's decree with unyielding precision, Daniel had intervened in the fate of a mortal man whose time on Earth had been cut short by human cruelty.

Without waiting for divine instruction, Daniel restored the man's life, believing it was the right thing to do. It wasn't rebellion, but rather an act of compassion and autonomy that stepped outside the bounds of God's will. Though God did not cast Daniel down with the fallen, He decreed that Daniel must atone for stepping beyond His perfect plan.

"Your heart is pure, Daniel, but your judgment was flawed," God had said. "You will descend to Earth, stripped of your celestial powers, to guide one of my children—a man who struggles to hear my voice. Only when he walks the path, I have set for him will your penance be complete."

David met Daniel during lunch a few days after his arrival. The cafeteria was bustling, and David noticed Daniel sitting alone, quietly bowing his head over his meal. Something about him drew David's attention, and he instinctively sat across from him.

"You new here?" David asked, breaking the silence.

Daniel looked up, his gaze calm and penetrating. "Just got here a couple of days ago. Name's Daniel."

David nodded. "David. What brought you here?"

Daniel smiled faintly. "A lot of things, I suppose. But mostly, I'm here to help."

David laughed lightly, mistaking the seriousness in Daniel's tone for humility. "Well, you picked the right place for that."

A New Friend

Over the next few days, Daniel quickly integrated himself into the mission's routine. He wasn't the loudest or most charismatic, but his presence was magnetic. He had a way of listening that made people feel truly heard, and his advice—always calm and measured—seemed to strike at the heart of every issue.

David found himself drawn to Daniel, spending hours talking with him. Daniel's perspective on life, faith, and struggle was unlike anyone David had ever met.

One evening, as they cleaned up after dinner, David asked, "You ever feel like there's something bigger going on? Like... all this pain and chaos, maybe it's not meaningless?"

Daniel paused, looking thoughtful. "I think everything has a purpose, even if we can't see it. Sometimes, the hardest struggles are shaping us for something greater."

David nodded, feeling the weight of those words. He didn't know why, but he trusted Daniel more than he trusted anyone in a long time.

What David couldn't see, was the subtle glow that sometimes appeared around Daniel when he was alone. It wasn't visible to the human eye, but it was a sign of his true nature—a messenger sent from

Heaven, not to perform miracles, but to guide David through the trials ahead.

Daniel himself wrestled with his mission. Though he knew the divine plan, he couldn't reveal it to David or directly intervene in the ways he was accustomed to as an angel. He was bound to the limits of his human form, forced to trust that God's wisdom would carry both him and David through.

There were moments, however, when Daniel's angelic nature slipped through. One night, as David sat awake in the dormitory, grappling with the despair that often crept in during the small hours, he glanced toward Daniel's bunk. For a split second, he thought he saw a faint shimmer around his friend, like a golden light flickering just beneath the surface. But when he blinked, it was gone.

"Must be my eyes playing tricks on me," David muttered, shaking his head. But deep down, he wondered if there was more to Daniel than met the eye.

TURNING POINT

Daniel knew that David was at a turning point. The spiritual attacks, the temptations, and the doubts were all part of the enemy's attempt to derail David from his destiny. What David didn't know, but Daniel could see clearly, was that David's path wasn't just about his own salvation—it was tied to something far greater.

Though bound by his earthly limitations, Daniel remained vigilant. He prayed in silence, watched over David, and prepared for the moment when his true purpose would be revealed. Until then, he would walk beside David, guiding him step by step through the storm.

UPHEAVAL

The forces in the demonic realm stirred, watching the delicate dance between good and evil as if it were a game to be won or lost. The Evil One, ever the patient strategist, had long been content to let his machinations unfold without interference. His servants, like Lilith, moved through the world as he had orchestrated, each with their own agenda, yet all working toward his ultimate goal. His power, vast and unchallenged, overshadowed everything in their realm. Lilith despised him, resented being his pawn, but her own power was nothing in comparison to his. She was bound by the necessity of serving him, like a slave to a cruel master, doing his bidding even when it clashed with her own desires.

What was unexpected, however, was Daniel's arrival.

Daniel was not just any mortal; he was something far more than that. Sent by God as both a penitent and a guide, he had entered the world without his heavenly power—a punishment and a mission all in one. His purpose was clear, even if David, the one he was meant to guide, would not yet understand the full significance of his presence. Daniel's very existence was an anomaly in the plan that had been set in motion. He wasn't meant to be there, not in the way he was.

For now, God watched in silence, allowing His plan to unfold at its own pace. The heavens were quiet, observing from a distance, biding their time. But in the depths of the demonic realm, things were not as still. The Evil One had his eye on Daniel, though he could not yet see the full scope of the plan that was unraveling before him. He had hoped for a smooth course, watching Lilith's influence stretch out to twist the world as he wished. But Daniel's unexpected arrival, his role as a protector to David, was a disruption he had not anticipated.

The Evil One was not a being of rashness. He knew better than to act too swiftly, but there was no denying the unease that rippled through the abyss. He had wanted things to play out quietly, as they always had, with souls slipping effortlessly into his domain. Now, the game had changed. Daniel, though unknowing of his own purpose, had already begun to influence the course of events. The Evil One would not allow this interference to continue unchecked. But he also knew that his time to act had not yet come—at least, not until the moment of decision was at hand. For now, he would wait, content in his knowledge that the battle was only just beginning.

In the meantime, Lilith seethed with anger, aware that her fate, too, was tied to the whims of the Evil One. She had no choice but to follow his orders, to watch as David's life unfolded with the weight of something larger than either of them could truly comprehend. But the presence of Daniel, this angel who walked among them as a mortal, was a threat—a disruption of the delicate balance that had been struck. And though she was forced to obey the Evil One, she couldn't help but them as a mortal, was a threat—a disruption of the delicate balance that had been struck. And though she was forced to obey the Evil One, she couldn't help but wonder: would Daniel's intervention prove to be her undoing?

God, meanwhile, watched with patience and resolve. His plan was long in the making, and while the Evil One moved his pieces with precision, He, too, had His own designs. The battle was one that would stretch across time, with every soul caught in the middle, each one playing their part in the grand story of redemption and destruction.

And Daniel, for all his confusion, would be at the heart of it all.

Past Times

David's mind often wandered back to the days after his brother Sean's death. The memory of those few agonizing hours in the hospital felt as sharp as ever. Sean had been in a coma for three days after the car accident, and David had stayed by his side, watching and praying, unwilling to leave his brother's side. But when the opportunity to go home, take a shower, and change clothes presented itself, David had seized it, thinking it would be a brief break—a moment to refresh himself before returning.

He had made it only a few blocks from the hospital when his phone rang. The doctor's voice was grave, telling David that Sean wasn't going to make it. David's heart dropped, but he tried to push the panic away and rushed back to the hospital as fast as he could. By the time he arrived, it was too late. The doctor stood at the ICU door and simply shook his head. Sean was already gone.

The weight of guilt hit David like a tidal wave. He had left his little brother alone to die. He had been so close, only minutes away, but he hadn't been there when it mattered. The shame of that moment haunted him. It was a painful reminder of the time he had left his father alone, too, when he had asked David to come with him on the night he passed. David had refused, wanting to stay in a hotel room, unwilling to face the uncomfortable realities of life on the streets. He never saw his father again, and that was a regret that gnawed at him as much as Sean's death did.

And then, there was his mother. She had passed away while David was locked up in Texas, unable to attend her funeral or even say goodbye. The loss of his family had left him feeling like an orphan, adrift in a sea of grief. Each death weighed heavily on him, and each time he failed to be there for the ones he loved, it added another burden to his already broken soul.

Weeks after Sean's funeral, David found himself at a mutual friend's house, Katrina's place. He had downloaded a ghost box app on his phone, something to distract his mind from the grief that lingered. He wasn't expecting anything real to happen, but when they began discussing Sean, something strange occurred.

The ghost box suddenly came to life, the static clearing long enough for a voice to say, "Sean."

David and Katrina exchanged wide-eyed glances. Neither of them had spoken Sean's name out loud. David quickly grabbed the phone and asked, "Sean?"

The ghost box responded, "Where am I?"

Then, in the midst of the static, one final word echoed through the phone— "Lost."

David felt a chill run through him, and though Katrina tried to console him, he couldn't shake the eerie feeling that something was terribly wrong. Was Sean's spirit lost, unable to find peace? Was he still trying to reach David, seeking something he couldn't explain? The moment left David with more questions than answers, and a sense of unresolved pain that gnawed at him.

Later, during a reading with a spiritual guide, David would be told that the ghostly presence he had encountered was not merely a manifestation of grief—it was something deeper. A sign of unresolved regret, a cry for redemption that lingered in the air like a cloud he couldn't shake.

As David's journey toward spiritual awakening continued, he would realize that his family's deaths were not random tragedies. They were part of something much larger—a divine plan he couldn't fully understand yet. And just like the encounter with the ghost box, there were signs and whispers from the beyond that would guide him toward his purpose. But first, he had to confront the haunting guilt and unanswered questions that bound him to the past.

David's sense of unease began long before the curandera's reading. The cryptic message from the fortune cookie, "The universe is trying to tell you something,"

hung heavy in his mind. It was a strange moment, eating at the back of his thoughts, and as much as he tried to ignore it, it lingered. It felt almost like an omen, a subtle message from something bigger than him, something beyond his understanding. He'd thought at the time that it was just a coincidence, something subtle message from something bigger than him, something beyond his understanding. He'd thought at the time that it was just a coincidence, something insignificant. But now, after hearing the curandera speak about two women—one representing love and family, the other representing anger and revenge—and then the mention of the person he had recently lost trying to communicate with him, it suddenly clicked.

Could this be the same message, the same warning that had come to him years ago in that Chinese restaurant, dressed up in different forms? Was the universe trying to prepare him for what was to come, to help him understand the strange dynamic in his relationship with Sandi and the darkness that had been slowly unfolding? Or, was it all connected to the loss of Sean, the shame he carried with him, and the unresolved guilt that gnawed at him?

The curandera had said someone was trying to reach him, and David now wondered if it was Sean, or even his mother or father, somehow trying to make amends, trying to guide him through this difficult, confusing time. The timing felt right, especially with everything happening with Sandi. He felt like he was standing on the precipice of something major, a revelation that could turn his life upside down and give him answers, but he didn't know where it would lead or if he was ready to hear it.

David had never been one to look for signs or believe in the mystical or supernatural, but there was a mounting pressure, a sense that something much larger than his circumstances was at play. He couldn't ignore the way his past seemed to be echoing into his present life, shaping his choices and relationships. And now, with Sandi's growing darkness, he was starting to believe that perhaps the universe was trying to tell him something much deeper than just the surface of things.

The thoughts of his brother, Sean, lingered heavily as well. The ghost box had said, "Where am I?" and "Lost." Those words haunted David, making him question if there was more to the death of his brother than he'd realized. He had been so caught up In his own pain, in the regret of not being there when Sean needed him, that he hadn't taken the time to reflect on the possibility that Sean's spirit was trying to communicate, to warn him of something.

Now, David couldn't help but wonder—what if it wasn't just the loss of Sean that had led him down this path? What if there were still threads tying him to the other side, pulling him toward something bigger than himself? What if the universe was trying to align these events, these people, and these messages to lead him to a truth about himself and his purpose that he had been too blind to see?

The weight of all these questions pressed on him, making him feel like he was caught in a cosmic web. But one thing was for sure—he couldn't ignore these signs any longer. He needed to understand what the universe, Sean, and whatever larger force was out there, was trying to tell him.

It was all so confusing, so many things to consider, so many people lost, all the struggle, the spiritual attacks, it was enough to drive him mad—where did it all fit in together. David's thoughts weighed heavily on him. He knelt down on aching knees and prayed to the Father to give him revelation, for guidance, for knowledge, but mostly for the wisdom to understand it all. The power of discernment was the one thing he always asked God to grant him, but it was as if it was the one thing he never received...at least not in the amount he longed for. His continual struggled to hear Gods voice.

A Meeting with Daniel

The kitchen was alive with the clatter of dishes and the comforting aroma of freshly baked bread. David worked silently beside Daniel, peeling potatoes, his hands moving almost mechanically while his mind churned over the fragments of his recent memories: Sean's voice, the fortune cookie, the curandera's cryptic words.

Daniel, as always, seemed at ease. His movements were deliberate, his presence calming. David glanced at him, debating whether to speak. Finally, he broke the silence.

"Do you believe in signs?" David asked, his voice low to avoid drawing attention from the others working nearby.

Daniel paused, setting down his knife. "I believe God communicates with us in many ways. Sometimes it's through scripture, sometimes through people, and sometimes in ways we don't expect. Why do you ask?"

David hesitated but then decided to open up. "A lot of weird things have happened in my life. Things that... feel connected. Like someone— or something—is trying to tell me something, but I don't know what. My brother passed away a few years back, and not long after, I got this... message. It was his voice, asking where he was. Then later, I got a fortune cookie that said, 'The universe is trying to tell you something.' I just don't get it. What's the point of sending messages I can't understand?"

Daniel looked thoughtful, his gaze steady and kind. "Maybe the point isn't to understand everything right away. Sometimes it's about faith—trusting that the answers will come when you're ready to receive them. Have you ever prayed about it?"

David shook his head. "Not really. I've always felt like... I'm too far gone for that. Like God wouldn't waste His time on me."

Daniel smiled faintly; his tone gentle but firm. "You're never too far gone. Remember the story of the prodigal son? God's grace doesn't have limits, David. Maybe these signs are His way of showing you that He's still here, waiting for you to turn to Him."

David nodded; his heart heavy but strangely comforted. "You think I should pray about it?"

"Yes," Daniel said. "And maybe tonight's Bible study will help. Sometimes the words we need to hear come when we least expect them."

The Physical Manifestation

That evening, David and Daniel sat side by side in the mission's small chapel, the air thick with the soft hum of murmured prayers. The group leader read from.

Ephesians 6:12: "For we wrestle not against flesh and blood, but against principalities, against powers, against the rulers of the darkness of this world..."

As the words echoed through the room, David felt an inexplicable heaviness settle over him, pressing on his chest like an unseen weight. His hands gripped the edges of the worn wooden pew, his breath shallow.

He glanced at Daniel, who seemed unbothered, listening intently to the scripture. David tried to shake off the feeling, convincing himself it was just fatigue. But then, he felt it—a distinct pressure on his shoulder, as though a hand had rested there.

Startled, he whipped his head around, but no one was behind him. His heart pounded, and he could feel the hair on his arms stand on end. The weight on his shoulder remained, firm and unrelenting.

David leaned toward Daniel, whispering, "Do you feel that?"

Daniel turned to him, his expression calm but serious. "Feel what?"

David hesitated, unsure of how to describe it. "It's like... someone's here. I feel it. Like a hand on my shoulder."

Daniel's eyes narrowed slightly, his demeanor shifting. He didn't dismiss David's claim; instead, he placed a hand on David's other shoulder. "Don't be afraid. If you're sensing something, it could mean the spiritual realm is closer than usual. Let's pray together after the study."

David nodded, but the unease lingered. As the session continued, he couldn't shake the feeling that something—or someone—was watching him.

When the study ended, Daniel pulled him aside. They knelt in one of the pews, and Daniel prayed softly, asking for protection and clarity for David. As he spoke, David felt the weight on his shoulder lift, replaced by an overwhelming sense of peace.

For the first time in a long time, David felt a glimmer of hope—an assurance that he wasn't alone in his struggles, that something greater was at work.

An Unexpected Visitor at the Mission

The Mission's dining hall was alive with its usual hum of conversation and clinking utensils as residents ate their evening meal. David was helping a newly arrived family—a single mother and her two young children—find their way to a bunk in the dormitory. Just as he returned to the hall, the front doors creaked open.

The man who entered stood out immediately. His face was gaunt, his movements deliberate, and his eyes—sharp, almost predatory—scanned the room as if searching for something. He introduced himself as Nathaniel and asked for a place to stay. The staff accommodated him, though David noticed a hesitation from Daniel, who lingered near the doorway as Nathaniel passed.

In the hours that followed, an unsettling shift swept through the Mission. Arguments erupted over simple matters—who had taken someone's seat, whose turn it was to use the shower. Residents who had been friendly earlier were now snapping at each other. David overheard snippets of conversations: people voicing regrets they'd buried long ago or speaking about personal pain they rarely shared.

David confided his concerns to Daniel, who seemed deeply troubled.

"Evil doesn't always announce itself," Daniel murmured. "Sometimes, it simply...amplifies what's already within. Keep an eye on him, David. And pray."

A Night Vision

The dormitory was quiet, the lights dimmed, but David couldn't sleep. His mind replayed the events of the day, and his unease about Nathaniel grew. Finally, exhaustion overtook him, and he drifted into a vivid dream.

He found himself on a vast plain under a sky choked with ash. Before him, angels and demons clashed in a chaotic, fiery battle. The ground trembled under the weight of their struggle.

David spotted Daniel, radiant in golden armor, wielding a blazing sword against a towering demon cloaked in shadow. "Stay behind me!" Daniel called, but David's feet were rooted, unable to move.

The shadows surged toward David; their whispers relentless: You abandoned your family. You're unworthy of redemption. The voices grew louder, surrounding him in a suffocating haze.

Just as he felt overwhelmed, Daniel's sword struck the ground, and a wave of light erupted, driving the shadows back. David awoke with a jolt, his chest heaving.

When he sat up, something caught his eye—a pristine white feather lying beside him. He picked it up, its softness like nothing he'd ever felt. It glowed faintly in the dim room, and he knew it was no ordinary feather.

The Revelation of Daniel's Past

The next morning, David found Daniel in the chapel, sitting in quiet prayer. The feather still in hand, David approached cautiously.

"I need to talk to you," he said, holding out the feather. "This was there when I woke up. After a dream."

Daniel studied the feather, his face unreadable. "Tell me about the dream," he said softly. David recounted the battle, the shadows, and Daniel's radiant light.

"What do you think it means?" David asked.

"That you're being called," Daniel replied. "But the question is—will you answer?"

David pressed further. "What are you not telling me, Daniel? You always seem to know more than you let on."

Daniel hesitated, then shared a glimpse of his past. He spoke of his time as a preacher, how pride had led him astray. He'd sought to build a church in his name, not God's, and when his congregation needed him most, he'd failed them.

"I lost my way," Daniel admitted. "And I was sent here—to atone, to guide. But my story doesn't matter as much as yours. Trust in the path you're being led to."

Lilith's Direct Confrontation

That evening, the chapel was cold, the air heavy with an unnatural stillness. David knelt in prayer, seeking guidance.

"Why do I feel so lost?" he whispered. "If there's a plan, why can't I see it?"

A chill swept through the room, and the shadows seemed to deepen. A voice, smooth and venomous, echoed through the air.

"Poor David," it mocked. "Always searching, always doubting. You think there's a grand design for you? There's nothing but the ruin you've made of your life."

David's heart raced as a dark figure materialized before him—a woman of otherworldly beauty with glowing, ember-like eyes.

"Lilith," he whispered, the name surfacing from some deep, instinctual part of him.

She smiled, a sharp, mocking grin. "You've caused quite the stir. But you're no match for what's coming. Your guilt, your shame—it will destroy you. And when it does, I'll be there to collect what's left."

Before David could respond, the chapel doors burst open, and Daniel entered. His presence filled the room with a calming but commanding energy.

"You have no claim here, Lilith," Daniel said firmly. "Leave."

Lilith hissed but began to fade, her form dissolving into the shadows. Before she disappeared completely, she whispered, "You can't protect him forever."

David turned to Daniel, shaken. "What just happened?" "Evil doesn't give up easily," Daniel said. "But you're stronger than you know. Trust in that."

God's Command and the Journey to the Mountains

The next evening, Daniel came to David with a solemn expression, his voice resonating with purpose.

"I've prayed for guidance," Daniel began. "God has shown me a glimpse of what's to come. You must go to the mountains, David. Alone. Build a fire there and pray. Someone will come to you."

David, though skeptical, felt an undeniable tug in his spirit—a pull stronger than doubt. "What happens if I don't?" he asked.

"This isn't just a calling, David. It's a directive," Daniel said firmly, his eyes searching David's for understanding. "Your obedience could shape more than just your path. It could shape everything."

The next morning, with little more than a canteen of water, a knife, and a lighter, David began his hike. The mountains loomed before him, their peaks cutting sharply into the sky. The air grew thinner as he ascended, each step bringing an odd mix of clarity and tension. By the time he reached a plateau that felt right, night had fallen. Stars speckled the vast heavens, their light piercing the velvety darkness.

THE ANGEL'S ARRIVAL

David gathered branches and lit a fire. The flames danced, casting flickering shadows across the jagged rocks. Kneeling beside the fire, he closed his eyes, praying clumsily, his words a mixture of desperation and uncertainty.

"God, I don't know what I'm supposed to do, but I'm here. If You're real, if You're listening...show me."

Hours passed, and exhaustion pulled at him. He fell asleep, curled near the fire for warmth.

When he awoke, it was not to the crackle of flames but to an overwhelming presence. The fire had dimmed, reduced to embers, and standing within the soft glow was a being of staggering magnificence.

The angel towered over him, clothed in robes of radiant light that shimmered with hues indescribable—gold, sapphire, and an ethereal white that seemed to bend reality itself. Six wings unfurled behind the angel, their feathers glistening like molten silver. Eyes like burning suns gazed at David, their intensity softened by an reality itself. Six wings unfurled behind the angel, their feathers glistening like molten silver. Eyes like burning suns gazed at David, their intensity softened by an undercurrent of compassion.

David trembled, his heart pounding against his ribs. "Who—what are you?" he stammered.

"Do not be afraid," the angel said, its voice a harmonious blend of countless tones, resonating not just in the air but deep within David's soul.

The angel stood silent for a moment; its head tilted as if listening to an unseen command. The silence pressed heavily upon David, almost suffocating, like an unseen force amplifying the weight of the moment. Then, the angel spoke again, its words vibrating with an energy that transcended sound, touching every corner of his being.

THE ANGEL'S MESSAGE

"This is a pivotal moment in your life, David," the angel said, its tone grave yet tinged with hope. "Upon this moment rests not just your future, but perhaps the course of the world itself. You are not merely called to a destiny—you are chosen for a transformation that will ripple through time and space."

David's breath caught as the angel continued. "This is not about you alone. You are being entrusted with knowledge so profound that it touches every corner of existence—a story woven through time and space, sewn into the hearts of the ones chosen to look behind the subterfuge. We are not just players but keepers of that story."

David felt his mind reel, a dizzying flood of questions surging forward. "Why me? I've made so many mistakes. I'm nobody!"

The angel's gaze softened. "God does not call the perfect, David. He perfects the called."

The angel's tone grew heavier, chilling. "There are forces at work—both mortal and divine—that have been locked in a struggle older than civilization itself. You believe the world is governed by nations, leaders, governments, wealth, influence...but you do not see the faction that dwells in the spaces between order and chaos."

David whispered, "A faction? Manipulating events?"

The angel nodded. "Yes, David. And you...you are the key to unraveling their schemes." But before the angel could explain further, a great rumbling shook the ground. The fire extinguished, plunging the night into pitch-blackness.

The Demonic Manifestation

David awoke with a jolt, his chest heaving. Daniel stood near him, his back to the fire's faint glow, his head whipping around as though searching for something.

"What's happening?" David cried, scrambling to his feet.

Before Daniel could respond, the ground began to crack beneath their feet, dark fissures radiating outward. From these openings emerged shadowy tendrils, writhing like living smoke, their touch chilling the air.

A voice, deep and guttural, reverberated from the darkness: "Did you think you could interfere without consequence? You will fail, David. You are nothing—just another broken man clinging to scraps of hope."

David froze, terror gripping him as the shadows began to take form —ghastly figures with hollow eyes and gaping maws. "Daniel, what do we do?"

Daniel turned; his face fierce. "Stand firm! Don't give in to fear!"

The voice laughed, a sound like grinding stones. "Your faith is weak, and your resolve weaker. You cannot stand against the ancient ones.".

David felt his legs buckle, but a surge of defiance welled within him. He clenched his fists, shouting into the darkness, "I'm not afraid of you!"

The figures recoiled slightly, as if struck by an unseen force. But the rumbling intensified, and David felt the ground giving way beneath him.

The Angel's Intervention

As the ground split further, the shadowy figures advanced, their forms twisting unnaturally. David's defiance began to waver, replaced by an overwhelming sense of vulnerability. The voice returned, dripping with malice.

"Do you see, David? Your strength is fleeting, your courage hollow. You cannot stand against us. Even now, your fears outweigh your faith."

David fell to his knees, his heart pounding as the tendrils of darkness encircled him. But before they could reach him, a brilliant light erupted from above. The angel descended once more, its presence banishing the darkness with an almost deafening hum of divine power.

"Enough!" the angel's voice thundered, shaking the very air.

The shadowy figures recoiled, writhing as if in agony. "You have no claim here," the angel proclaimed. "This man is under divine protection, chosen for a purpose far beyond your reach."

The angel extended a radiant hand toward David, pulling him to his feet. "Do not fear, David. Your strength lies not in yourself but in the One who has called you.

Stand firm and trust."

David felt an indescribable warmth flood his body—a sensation of peace and courage replacing his terror. The tendrils of darkness disintegrated, leaving only the jagged cracks in the earth.

The angel turned to David; its gaze intense but kind. "This was only the beginning. Forces greater than these will try to sway you, to make you doubt. But remember this moment. Remember who you are and whose you are."

David nodded, tears streaming down his face. "I understand now. But...why me? Why would God choose someone as broken as I am?"

The angel smiled; a gesture so profound it seemed to illuminate the entire mountainside. "Broken vessels often hold the most light. Your pain, your trials—they have prepared you for this. Through you, others will find hope."

THE DEMONIC THREAT

Before the angel could continue, the demonic voice echoed again, fainter but filled with venom.

"This isn't over, David. You may have divine favor, but the world will test you. Your past will haunt you. And when you falter, we will be there, waiting."

The angel raised a hand, silencing the voice with a burst of light. "You have no power here." "Back to the depths of Hell," the angel's voice boomed!

The cracks in the ground began to close, sealing the darkness below. The angel placed a hand on David's shoulder, its touch radiating reassurance. "Go now.

Return to the world, but do not forget what you have seen and heard. Your journey will not be easy, but you are not alone."

Awakening in Reality

David jolted awake, his chest heaving. The fire had gone out, and the first rays of dawn painted the sky in hues of orange and gold. Daniel sat nearby, his back to David, staring into the distance.

"You saw it too, didn't you?" David whispered.

Daniel turned; his expression unreadable. "I felt it," he replied. "The ground shaking, the darkness...whatever just happened, it wasn't just a dream."

David looked down at his hands, trembling but alive with a new purpose. "We're in the middle of something bigger than we can imagine."

Daniel nodded solemnly. "Then let's make sure we're ready for it."

The First Revelation

David sat alone in the room of a small library he had stumbled upon during one of his long walks. The angel's words about profound knowledge echoed in his mind like a puzzle he couldn't solve. As he scanned the rows of dusty books, his attention was drawn to an ancient-looking tome, its leather cover worn with age but emanating an odd warmth when he touched it.

The book seemed to vibrate in his hands as he opened it, the script inside written in a language he couldn't understand. Yet, as he stared at the text, the letters shifted and rearranged themselves, transforming into words he could read. The book spoke of a "Covenant of the Chosen," a group of souls predestined to safeguard a hidden truth that had been passed down through ages.

David's heart raced as the text described his life in cryptic detail—the struggles, the losses, the moments of despair—and pointed to his role in a plan that spanned time itself. A phrase stood out: "To uncover the truth, one must see beyond the veil of pain." At that moment, he felt a searing heat on his chest, where a mark began to form—a sigil glowing faintly before fading into his skin.

A Return to the Past

The revelation triggered a flood of memories. David was thrust into vivid recollections of his past, moments that seemed ordinary but now carried a deeper meaning. He remembered Sean's death, the haunting regret of not being there in his brother's final moments. As the memory replayed, he noticed something new —a faint light near Sean's hospital bed, as if someone unseen had been with him in those final moments.

Another memory surfaced, this time of his father asking him to come along that fateful night. For years, David had carried the guilt of refusing, but now he saw the scene differently. A shadowy figure loomed near his father as he walked away, its presence ominous. David realized it was no coincidence—forces had been manipulating events in his life, steering him toward this very moment.

His mother's death while he was in prison replayed in his mind next. He had always assumed it was just another cruel twist of fate, but now he saw flashes of a glowing presence in his prison cell, as though someone had been watching over him, silently guiding him through his despair.

Daniel's Similar Story

David, shaken by his revelations, sought out Daniel, needing answers. He found Daniel in the dimly lit kitchen of their shared space, sipping tea and staring into the distance.

"Daniel, I need to know something. Have you ever... felt like your life wasn't your own? Like you were being steered toward something?" David's voice was raw with urgency.

Daniel hesitated, his hands trembling slightly as he set his cup down. "David, there's something I've been meaning to tell you. I wasn't always... here."

He went on to describe a near-death experience years ago when a car accident left him teetering between life and death. During those fleeting moments, Daniel claimed to have seen an otherworldly figure bathed in light, who spoke of a great purpose he would one day fulfill. Since then, Daniel had experienced strange visions and an inexplicable pull toward David, though he didn't understand why until now.

"Everything I've been through," Daniel said, his voice barely above a whisper, "was to prepare me to help you. I didn't realize it until recently, but I've been... chosen, too."

The Faction Reveals Itself

Their conversation was interrupted by a sudden chill that swept through the room. The lights flickered, and a low growl echoed from the shadows. Daniel stood abruptly, his eyes darting around the room.

"They're here," he said, his voice sharp with fear.

From the darkness emerged figures cloaked in shadow, their forms shifting and writhing as if made of smoke. One stepped forward, its voice like nails scraping against steel.

"You think you can unravel the tapestry, mortal?" it hissed. "You're nothing but a pawn in a game far beyond your comprehension."

David felt the ground beneath him tremble, the air growing thick with an oppressive energy. Daniel stepped in front of him, his face set with determination. "They're trying to stop you, David. They're afraid of what you'll discover."

The shadowy figure laughed; a sound devoid of humor. "Afraid? No. You're but an inconvenience. The truth you seek will be your undoing."

Test of Faith and Resolve

In the days that followed, David was haunted by doubt. He questioned whether he was strong enough to face the forces arrayed against him. The sigil on his chest burned faintly, a constant reminder of the burden he carried.

One night, he encountered a homeless man who asked for help. David had little to give, but he shared his meal and listened to the man's story. The man spoke of losing everything but still finding strength in his faith. "Sometimes," he said, "it's not about what you can do for yourself, but what you can do for others."

The encounter reignited David's resolve. He realized that his journey wasn't just about uncovering the truth—it was about becoming the kind of person who could carry that truth, no matter the cost.

Later, he faced a more dire test. A mysterious figure offered him a chance to undo his past mistakes: to save Sean, to be there for his father, to prevent his mother's death. All it would cost was his current path. David struggled, the temptation almost unbearable, but he ultimately refused, understanding that his suffering had shaped him into who he was meant to be.

SCOTT'S GOODBYE

David was outside the small cabin when Scott approached him. The air was still, the mountains behind them bathed in the golden light of dusk. Scott's face was solemn, his hands tucked into the pockets of his worn jacket. David, sensing something, looked up from the firewood he was stacking.

"You've got that look," David said, half-joking. "What's on your mind?"

Scott exhaled deeply; his breath visible in the cooling air. "I wanted to talk to you before I left."

David froze mid-motion, his brow furrowing. "Left? What do you mean?"

"I've been feeling it for a while now," Scott said, his voice steady but tinged with an unfamiliar weight. "I think my part in this... journey, or whatever you want to call it, is coming to an end. At least here. There's this pull I can't explain, David. I feel like I'm needed somewhere else."

David's chest tightened. "You're serious about this?"

Scott nodded, his eyes meeting David's. "Yeah. It's not that I want to leave you, man. It's just... something bigger than me is calling. It's like... they tell me what to do, where to go. I don't even know who 'they' are, but it's clear. I have to follow it."

David let the words sink in. "You're talking about divine guidance, aren't you? Like what I've been dealing with?"

"Exactly," Scott said. "Ever since the faction revealed itself, I've felt like I was a piece of the puzzle, but not the centerpiece. My path isn't here anymore. It's somewhere out there."

David clenched his jaw, wrestling with the realization that Scott—his steadfast companion through so much—was truly leaving. "What if I need you? You're my anchor, man."

Scott placed a hand on David's shoulder. "You're stronger than you think. You've been the one leading this charge, whether you realize it or not. My leaving doesn't change that."

The silence between them stretched, heavy with unspoken words. Finally, Scott broke it. "Remember what the angel said—this isn't just about us. It's about something far greater. If we're meant to cross paths again, we will."

David's throat tightened, but he nodded. "You'll be okay?"

Scott smiled faintly. "I don't know what's waiting for me out there, but I trust it's where I'm supposed to be."

They stood together a moment longer before Scott turned to walk away. David watched him disappear into the twilight, feeling the weight of both loss and gratitude.

DAVID'S REFLECTION

David processes Scott's departure, wondering if he's truly prepared for what lies ahead without him. This could lead into a moment of self-doubt but ultimately refocuses David's resolve. David adds another log to the fire, representing his decision to keep pushing forward, even as people he cares for move on.

THE VISION

David stirred in his sleep, restless. The flickering shadows from the embers of the dying fire seemed to dance across the walls of the cabin. In his dream, he was back at the motel room he once shared with Sandi. The air was thick with the same bittersweet memories—the sound of her laughter, the way she used to touch his face, the warmth of her presence.

But something was off.

Sandi appeared before him, wearing the familiar mischievous smile that always made his heart race. She moved toward him, her voice a siren's call, soft and alluring. "David," she whispered, her touch feather-light on his arm. "I've missed you. Haven't you missed me?"

David felt an ache deep within him, a yearning he thought he had buried. Her hands slid over his shoulders as she leaned closer, her breath warm against his skin. But as her lips brushed his, something inside him recoiled. Her touch was too cold, her voice too sweet, as if dipped in poison.

He pulled back, staring into her eyes. They weren't Sandi's. The soft brown he remembered had been replaced with an unnatural, burning red. Her smile twisted into something predatory, and her voice deepened, dripping with malice. "What's the matter, David? Don't you want me? After all, I'm everything you've ever desired."

Suddenly, the room shifted. The walls dissolved into a void, leaving only David and the entity before him. She transformed, her beauty giving way to an otherworldly terror. Her features elongated, her skin pale and cracked like porcelain. Wings—dark and leathery—unfurled from her back.

"Lilith," David whispered, his voice trembling.

She laughed, a sound that echoed through the emptiness. "You're more perceptive than I thought. But it's too late. You're already mine."

David felt a crushing weight on his chest as she advanced, her hands clawing at him, trying to pull him into the abyss. Desperation filled him. "No!" he cried out, his voice a plea into the void. "Daniel! Help me!"

Daniel's Intervention

A blinding light erupted in the darkness, piercing through the shadows like a sword. Lilith hissed, recoiling as the figure of Daniel stepped forward, radiant and fierce. His human guise melted away, revealing his angelic form. His eyes burned with the intensity of a thousand suns, his golden wings stretching wide, their edges shimmering with divine fire.

"Back, Lilith!" Daniel commanded, his voice resonating with power. "You have no claim here."

Lilith snarled, her form writhing as she resisted the light. "This one is already ensnared. He has walked too far in the darkness."

Daniel stepped between her and David, shielding him. "He is not yours. His soul is claimed by the Most High."

Lilith lunged, her claws outstretched, but Daniel raised his hand. A wave of light surged from him, striking her. She screamed, her form disintegrating into shadowy tendrils that fled into the void. The darkness dissolved, and David found himself back in the cabin, gasping for air.

AFTERMATH

Daniel stood over David, his expression a mix of concern and authority. "Are you alright?"

David sat up, trembling. "What...what was that?"

"Lilith," Daniel said, his tone grave. "She has been watching you, waiting for a moment of weakness. Tonight, she tried to claim you."

David buried his face in his hands, his voice shaking. "I almost fell for it. I thought she was Sandi."

Daniel knelt beside him, placing a reassuring hand on his shoulder. "Do not blame yourself. The enemy knows our deepest wounds and uses them against us.

But you called out for help, David. That is what matters."

David looked up, his eyes filled with both fear and determination. "Why me, Daniel? Why does all of this keep happening to me?"

Daniel's gaze softened. "Because you are chosen, David. Your path is not easy, but it is vital. The forces of darkness will do everything in their power to derail you. But you are not alone. Trust in the One who called you, and trust in yourself."

David nodded slowly, the gravity of the moment sinking in. He knew now that the battle ahead would test him in ways he couldn't yet imagine. But he also knew he wouldn't face it alone.

The Aftermath: The Angel's Transformation As the suffocating silence faded and David's labored breathing began to slow, Daniel remained by his side, his angelic form still radiant. The warmth of the light emanating from his wings filled the cabin, dispelling every trace of shadow and fear. Daniel knelt over David, concern etched on his face, as the golden glow around him pulsed like a heartbeat.

But then, the radiance began to dim. The fiery brilliance of Daniel's wings flickered, retracting into his back like embers retreating into ash. His celestial armor melted away, replaced by his familiar human clothing. His posture softened, his presence grounding itself back in the mortal realm. David, unconscious from the overwhelming encounter, slumped onto the floor, his body trembling faintly as though caught in the aftershocks of a divine storm.

Daniel looked down at David, his expression heavy with compassion and sorrow. "Forgive me," he whispered, his voice tinged with regret. "It is not yet time for you to see me as I truly am."

He leaned closer, brushing his hand lightly over David's forehead. "Sleep now," Daniel murmured, his words laced with a soft, otherworldly cadence. "Let the memory of tonight's revelation fade, for the weight of its truth would crush you before you are ready. But take heart, for your soul is stronger than you know."

DAVID AWAKENS

When David finally stirred, the cabin was still. The fire had long since burned down to a bed of glowing embers, their faint warmth a stark contrast to the intensity of the dream—or was it a dream? His head pounded, and his body felt as though it had been wrung dry of every ounce of energy.

He sat up slowly, looking around. There was no sign of the battle that had just taken place, no trace of Lilith or the blinding light that had banished her. His heart raced as he tried to piece together what had happened. The last thing he remembered was crying out for help, and then... nothing. Just darkness.

"David?" Daniel's voice broke through his thoughts. He turned to see his friend sitting in the corner, his back against the wall, his face pale and drawn.

"Daniel," David said, his voice hoarse. "What happened? I—there was something—someone—" He faltered, the memories slipping through his grasp like water through his fingers.

Daniel shook his head gently, his eyes filled with quiet understanding. "You were dreaming, David. A nightmare, by the sound of it. But it's over now."

David stared at him, searching for answers in his friend's calm demeanor. Something about Daniel felt... different. There was a weight to his presence, an unspoken intensity that David couldn't quite place. But the more he tried to focus on it, the more his thoughts seemed to blur.

"Maybe," David said finally, though his voice lacked conviction. He glanced at the faint glow of the embers. "It felt so real."

"Sometimes," Daniel said, "our minds use dreams to process things we don't understand. But the important thing is that you're safe."

David nodded, though unease lingered at the edges of his mind. He couldn't shake the feeling that something monumental had just happened, something he couldn't remember. But for now, he let it go, too exhausted to dwell on it.

Daniel's Reflection

As David drifted back to sleep, Daniel sat in silence, his thoughts a tempest. He hadn't expected God to restore his angelic form, even temporarily. For centuries, he had walked the earth as a man, his true identity hidden beneath the veneer of humanity. To have his powers returned, even for a moment, was both a blessing and a burden.

He thought of the battle with Lilith, of the moment he had stood between David and the abyss. The memory of her hissed words still echoed in his mind: He is already ensnared. Daniel clenched his fists, his resolve hardening. He wouldn't allow that to happen. Not to David. Not to the one chosen for a purpose so vital, so profound, that even he didn't fully understand it.

But David wasn't ready to know the truth—not about Daniel, not about himself, and certainly not about the battle raging around him. In time, the veil would be lifted. Until then, Daniel would remain by his side, guiding him as best he could.

"Sleep well, David," he whispered, his voice barely audible over the crackling embers. "The road ahead is long, and the trials are only just beginning."

David's Restlessness and the Call to Eddy

After the events with Lilith and the angel's transformation, David finds himself in a strange and uneasy calm. The weight of his vision lingers in his mind, leaving him with unanswered questions. He wakes up feeling both awed and burdened, the memory of Daniel's angelic intervention only half-formed in his mind.

David's unease grows as he experiences vivid, fragmented dreams. He sees unfamiliar faces, scattered across vast, barren landscapes, each illuminated by a dim light fighting against the consuming shadows. A voice, distant but familiar, echoes: "Find them. The time is near."

The sense of urgency gnaws at him. Daniel, ever enigmatic, begins subtly guiding David toward his next step. One night, as they sit by a fire, Daniel brings up Eddy, almost as if reading David's thoughts.

Daniel: "There's a man you know. A friend from your past. He reached out to you, didn't he? You've been ignoring his call."

David is taken aback. "You mean Eddy?

Daniel doesn't answer directly but instead looks to the horizon; his silence more instructive than words. David knows then that he needs to reach out. He calls Eddy, his voice trembling as he speaks, and Eddy, far from surprised, says he's been expecting this call.

Eddy: "I knew you'd call eventually, man. I don't know what's going on, but... I think I need you here just as much as you need me."

THE JOURNEY

David embarks on the trip, his heart heavy with anticipation and doubt. Along the way, strange occurrences seem to follow him. Shadowy figures appear in the periphery of his vision, whispers in unknown tongues fill the silence during his quiet moments, and a growing sense of being watched settles over him.

When David arrives, Eddy greets him with a mix of relief and curiosity. Eddy shares his own experiences—visions of David and others, dreams that seem too real, and an unshakable feeling that their fates are intertwined. Together, they begin to piece together the fragments of their experiences, realizing they are part of something far greater than themselves.

THE FACTION MOVES

Unbeknownst to David and Eddy, their reunion has not gone unnoticed. The faction—agents of the unseen forces opposing the chosen ones—has been watching them closely. These beings, neither fully mortal nor fully divine, are tasked with preventing the chosen ones from uniting. They operate in the spaces between light and shadow, manipulating events to sow doubt, fear, and division.

One night, while David and Eddy are discussing their visions, the temperature in the room drops suddenly. The air grows heavy, oppressive, and they feel an otherworldly presence. David, recalling his vision of Lilith, stiffens.

Eddy: "Do you feel that? It's like... something's here."

Before David can answer, a mirror shatters, and a voice, deep and resonant, fills the room: "You think you can fight what has been since the beginning? You are fools, playing a game, you cannot win."

The lights flicker, and shadowy tendrils emerge from the walls, writhing toward them. David and Eddy stand frozen in fear until a burst of light fills the room. Daniel appears, his human form glowing faintly with divine energy, and the shadows retreat with an ear-piercing wail.

Daniel's Warning

After the incident, Daniel reveals more of the faction's nature. He explains that they are not mere mortals but ancient entities who have been working against the divine plan since time began. "Who are they", David asked? Daniel replies, "The Sons of Belial."

Daniel explains, "These beings are masters of deception. Agents of Chaos. They hide in plain sight, influencing governments, leaders, and even the hearts of men. They aim to prevent you and the others from fulfilling your purpose because they know what is at stake."

David and Eddy are shaken but resolute. Daniel advises them to be vigilant, for the faction will not stop. He also hints that they are not alone and that others like them are scattered across the world, waiting to be found.

A Test of Faith

The next night, David and Eddy decide to journey to a nearby mountain range Daniel mentioned. The hike is grueling, and the path seems to shift unnaturally, as if the mountain itself is resisting their presence. They finally reach a clearing where they are met with a stunning yet foreboding sight: an ancient altar, weathered by time but emanating a faint glow.

As they approach, the ground trembles, and shadowy figures begin to emerge. This time, there is no retreat, and David and Eddy must stand their ground. David recalls Daniel's earlier words about faith and courage, summoning his strength to pray aloud.

David: "I will not falter. I will not run. If I am chosen, then I choose to fight."

The figures hesitate, their forms wavering, and a blinding light erupts from the altar. The shadows dissipate, and David feels a warmth unlike anything he's known before—a confirmation that he is on the right path.

Visions within Visions

As they descend the mountain, David has another vision. He sees himself standing with a group of individuals, each distinct but united by a shared purpose. He recognizes Eddy among them and realizes this is only the beginning.

Daniel, waiting for them at the base of the mountain, confirms this. "The others will find you when the time is right. Until then, prepare yourselves. The battle is coming."

INTERVENTION

After David's harrowing encounter with Lilith and the divine intervention that saved him, he began to feel restless. The events, though surreal, left an undeniable imprint on his spirit. He felt as if unseen eyes were watching him at every moment. His connection with Daniel, though comforting, only seemed to intensify his sense that a storm was gathering, both within and without.

Daniel, always calm and deliberate, watched David struggle with the weight of these events. One evening, while they sat around a modest fire pit outside the New Life Rescue Mission, Daniel subtly nudged David toward action.

That night, as Eddy and David shared dinner in Eddy's modest apartment, strange phenomena began. The temperature in the room seemed to drop suddenly.

The lights flickered, and Eddy's dog, an old Labrador named Rosie, growled at the empty corner of the room.

"You feel that?" Eddy asked, his voice low.

David nodded. "Yeah. Something's here."

The First Encounter with Human Agents of the Faction

Unknown to David and Eddy, their growing alliance had attracted attention—not from demonic spirits, but from a group of master Satanists deeply embedded in the region. This faction, a secretive cult that blended ancient rites with modern influence, had been watching for signs of divine activity. When David's presence was confirmed through their rituals, they began to act.

One night, as David and Eddy sat talking in the living room, a loud crack sounded outside. They rushed to the window to find a crude effigy burning on the lawn — a grotesque figure made of twisted branches and animal bones, its center marked with an inverted pentagram.

"Get back!" Daniel shouted, appearing suddenly, his face tense.

Before David could respond, the effigy exploded in a burst of sulfuric smoke, filling the air with an acrid stench.

A Mission to the Mountains

Daniel, unusually grave, took David aside after the attack. "We need to go to the mountains," he said. "There's something you need to see. And it's not safe here."

David hesitated. "The mountains? Why?"

"You'll understand when we get there. But you have to trust me."

The next day, the three men—David, Daniel, and Eddy—left for the Rockies. Daniel led them deep into the wilderness, eventually stopping at a natural clearing surrounded by jagged cliffs. There, David noticed a circle of ancient stones forming a crude altar.

"Build a fire," Daniel instructed. "And sit. Pray."

David did as he was told, lighting the fire and offering a prayer. Hours passed, and as the flames died down, David felt himself drift into a strange half-sleep.

David's Vision: A Test of Faith

David's vision began subtly—a soft, unnatural glow emanating from the altar. Then, he saw a man approaching, his face obscured. But as the figure came closer, it shifted, transforming into Sandi's form. She smiled seductively, her voice a honeyed whisper.

"David," she purred. "Why fight this? You can have it all—me, peace, freedom. Just say yes."

But something in her eyes betrayed her. They were too dark, too cold. David recoiled. "You're not Sandi!" he shouted.

The figure snarled, Its form distorting. Shadows poured from its mouth as it lunged at him. David screamed, and suddenly, a blinding light erupted. Daniel stood over him, but not as the man David knew. Wings of radiant gold spread from his back, and his eyes burned with divine fire.

"Enough!" Daniel commanded, his voice shaking the earth.

The creature writhed, hissing in pain, before vanishing into smoke. David collapsed, unconscious.

Aftermath: A Quiet Awakening

When David woke, the sun was rising. He saw Daniel sitting by the fire, once again in his human form.

"What happened?" David asked.

"You had a nightmare," Daniel said simply, his tone calm but hiding something deeper.

David frowned, sensing there was more, but Daniel offered no further explanation.

Nearby, Eddy stared at Daniel with a newfound respect—and fear. Whatever had happened, it left a mark on all of them.

Daniel's Message to David: Letting Go so as to Embrace God's Plan

Daniel sat beside David one evening, the stars above seeming to press closer, their light illuminating the deep shadows of the mountains. Daniel's demeanor was calm yet purposeful, and his eyes carried the weight of divine revelation.

"David," Daniel began, his voice steady, "I have been instructed to share something with you—a message from God. Your struggles to hear His voice, to truly feel His guidance, stem from a weight you continue to carry. Picture your life like a garden. You've planted seeds of faith, of spiritual growth, and they have the potential to flourish. But for them to take root, you must first clear away the debris of the past."

David looked at Daniel intently, his brow furrowed as the words struck a chord deep within him.

"The struggles you've faced," Daniel continued, "the sorrow, the guilt, the doubt, the loneliness, the betrayals—they were all lessons. They served their purpose.

They were never meant to destroy you, David. They were meant to transform you, to refine you into the person God always knew you could be. Letting go doesn't mean forgetting; it means creating. It's about self-love, about trusting God's plan. Faith carried you through the storm, and it will carry you into the next phase of your life. Let faith be your compass."

David's breath caught as Daniel's words sank in, but Daniel wasn't finished.

"Honor the trials you've endured by letting them go. To hold on to them is to stifle the growth God has planned for you. Let go of the past—not to erase it, but to create something greater. Faith, resilience, and love—these are the tools you've been given. Use them to build the life God has waiting for you."

Scripture Supporting the Message

Daniel reached for his Bible, turning its well-worn pages with reverence. "God has always provided wisdom for those willing to listen. Let me share with you His word that reinforces this message."

1. Isaiah 43:18-19: "Forget the former things; do not dwell on the past. See, I am doing a new thing! Now it springs up; do you not perceive it? I am making a way in the wilderness and streams in the wasteland.

Daniel explained, "God reminds us that holding on to the past can blind us to the new opportunities He is creating."

2. Philippians 3:13-14: "Brothers and sisters, I do not consider myself yet to have taken hold of it. But one thing I do: Forgetting what is behind and straining toward what is ahead, I press on toward the goal to win the prize for which God has called me heavenward in Christ Jesus."

"Paul knew the importance of letting go," Daniel said. "His focus was on the future, not the burdens of the past."

3. 2 Corinthians 12:9: "But he said to me, 'My grace is sufficient for you, for my power is made perfect in weakness.' Therefore, I will boast all the more gladly about my weaknesses, so that Christ's power may rest on me."

"Your trials, David, are a testament to God's grace. Even in your weakest moments, He has been there, preparing you for this transformation."

4. Psalm 55:22: "Cast your cares on the Lord and he will sustain you; he will never let the righteous be shaken."

Daniel's voice softened. "Let go of what burdens you, David. Place it in God's hands."

DAVID'S REACTION

David's heart was heavy, but Daniel's words felt like a lifeline. Tears welled up in his eyes as he spoke. "I don't know how to let it go," he confessed. "The guilt, the pain—it's all I've known."

Daniel placed a reassuring hand on his shoulder. "You start by surrendering it to God, piece by piece. Pray, David. Trust. And when the weight begins to lift, you'll hear His voice clearer than ever."

David nodded, his resolve slowly building. He knelt by the fire, whispering a prayer. For the first time, the memories of his past didn't feel like chains. They felt like stones, finally being laid down.

The Great Commission

The campfire burned low, casting dancing shadows against the backdrop of the mountains. David sat with Daniel, listening intently as Daniel began to speak about a new revelation. His tone was serious, but his words carried the same comforting authority that David had come to recognize as divinely inspired.

"David," Daniel began, "there's something I need to share with you—a mission greater than yourself, greater than even the trials you've endured. It's the mission we are all called to as the chosen of God."

Daniel leaned forward; his face illuminated by the fire's glow. "Have you ever heard of the Great Commission?"

David nodded hesitantly. "It's about spreading God's word, right?"

"Yes," Daniel said, his voice firm. "But it's more than that. The Great Commission is a divine mandate, given to all who follow Christ. It's recorded in Matthew 28:18-20, where Jesus said:

'All authority in heaven and on earth has been given to me. Therefore, go and make disciples of all nations, baptizing them in the name of the Father and of the Son and of the Holy Spirit, and teaching them to obey everything I have commanded you. And surely, I am with you always, to the very end of the age.'

"These words were spoken by Christ to His disciples before He ascended into heaven. But they weren't just meant for them—they were meant for us, for all believers, for all time."

The Weight of the Commission

David felt a chill run down his spine as Daniel's words settled over him. "I've never thought of it that way," David admitted. "I always felt like I wasn't... worthy of something so big."

Daniel gave a gentle smile. "None of us are worthy on our own. That's the beauty of God's grace. The Great Commission isn't about being perfect—it's about being willing. It's about trusting God to work through us, even in our imperfection."

He paused and looked David in the eye. "You've been through hell and back. You've felt pain, loss, betrayal. But those experiences didn't break you—they prepared you. Who better to spread God's love than someone who has truly known the depths of His mercy?"

David was silent, the weight of Daniel's words pressing on him.

A Personal Call

Daniel continued, his tone growing more intense. "God has chosen you, David, not just to fight against the darkness, but to bring light to others. You've been given a unique perspective, a testimony that can reach people in ways others can't. You've lived it—God's redemption, His grace, His power to transform a broken life.

"But the Great Commission isn't just about telling people about God. It's about living it. It's about being a reflection of His love, His forgiveness, His justice. It's about showing people that even in the darkest times, God is there."

David's eyes glistened with unshed tears. "How? How do I even begin?"

"You already have," Daniel replied with a smile. "Every step you take in faith, every person you show kindness to, every word of hope you share—it's all part of the mission. And as you grow in faith, God will show you more. He'll guide you to the people who need to hear your story, who need to see His light through you."

The conversation shifted as Daniel revealed a vision he'd been given. "Soon, you'll face a choice," he said gravely. "A moment where your faith will be tested. The enemy will try to distract you, to convince you that you're not ready, that you're not enough. But remember this: God does not call the equipped. He equips the called. "And David," Daniel added, his voice dropping to a near whisper, "you have been called."

The Call to Action

That night, as David lay under the stars, he couldn't sleep. Daniel's words echoed in his mind, mingling with his own doubts and fears. Could he truly be part of something so significant? Could God really use someone like him?

Closing his eyes, David prayed. "God, I don't know what I'm doing. I don't know how to do this. But if You want me to, I'll try. Show me the way."

In that moment, a sense of peace washed over him, as if the very heavens had answered. And deep within his soul, he felt the quiet but unmistakable reassurance: You are not alone.

The Denver morning was brisk, the kind of cold that hinted at the coming winter. David zipped up his jacket as he joined Daniel, Eddy, and the others near the front of NLRM, New Life Rescue Mission's bustling shelter. In the early light, their breath turned to fog as they loaded boxes of Christian literature into the back of a beat-up van.

Eddy, ever the planner, directed the team. "Alright, everyone knows their routes. The goal is to spread the Word and offer some hope where it's needed most. Stay together, keep it peaceful, and remember **Isaiah 52:7**:

'How beautiful on the mountains are the feet of those who bring good news, who proclaim peace, who bring good tidings, who proclaim salvation, who say to Zion, "Your God reigns!"

David looked around at the team. There was Loyd, a cheerful bear of a man whose massive arms looked like they could snap a tree trunk; Tree, a gangly, six-and-a-half-foot-tall man whose deep voice carried authority; and the small but wiry Jason, a ball of energy who couldn't seem to stay still.

"This is the army, huh?" David said with a grin.

Daniel clapped him on the shoulder. "God's army doesn't need to be big. It just needs to be willing."

A Day in the Field

Their first stop was a neighborhood park. The group spread out, handing out small booklets, engaging in conversations, and praying with anyone who was willing. The mood was lighthearted but purposeful. David found himself growing more confident with each interaction, sharing his story of redemption and faith.

At one point, Jason darted up to him, out of breath. "Man, this is incredible! You see that guy over there? Just prayed for him—he's been homeless for years, but he's ready to come to the Mission. Says he's tired of running!"

David smiled, feeling a deep sense of fulfillment. For the first time in a long while, he felt like he was truly living for something bigger than himself.

The Encounter

As the sun dipped lower in the sky, the team moved to a rougher part of town. The atmosphere shifted. The streets seemed quieter; the people warier. Daniel noticed it too and signaled for the group to stay close.

It wasn't long before trouble found them. A group of men emerged from a nearby alley, their faces shadowed by hooded jackets. There were five of them, and their demeanor was anything but friendly.

"Hey, Bible thumpers," one of them sneered. "You think you can just walk in here and preach your fairy tales?"

Eddy stepped forward, his voice calm but firm. "We're just here to share some hope, brother. No need for trouble."

The leader laughed, a harsh, guttural sound. "Trouble? Oh, I think you brought trouble with you."

As if on cue, the men drew weapons—knives, chains, and makeshift clubs Continuation of the Scene As the adrenaline began to fade, the group leaned against a nearby wall, catching their breath. David looked at Daniel, a question burning in his eyes. "They weren't just street thugs, were they?" Daniel shook his head slowly. "No, David. They were sent."

"Sent? By who?" Jason piped up, still bouncing slightly on his toes.

"Not who—what," Daniel clarified. "These are pawns in a much larger game. They don't even realize they're being used by the faction."

David's mind raced, the fight replaying in his head. "The faction," he muttered, almost to himself. "I thought they were... spiritual, not human."

"They are both," Daniel said gravely. "There are forces at work in the spiritual realm that manipulate those in the physical world. These men, willingly or not, are tools of something much darker."

Loyd, still flexing his knuckles from the fight, let out a deep breath. "Well, if they come at us again, they're gonna need more than chains and knives."

Tree chuckled, his deep voice echoing off the nearby buildings. "Amen to that."

REFLECTION AND RENEWAL

As the group loaded back into the van, the mood was somber but resolute. Eddy, who had been quiet throughout the encounter, finally spoke. "You know, this isn't the first time I've seen something like this. Back when I first found my faith, I had a run-in with some people who seemed... off. I didn't know it then, but I see now they were under the same influence."

Daniel nodded. "The enemy will always try to intimidate those who are spreading the truth. But remember, fear is their greatest weapon—and our greatest weakness. That's why we must remain rooted in faith."

As they drove back to NLRM, Daniel turned to David. "You're starting to see it now, aren't you? The way the physical and spiritual worlds are intertwined."

David nodded. "Yeah, but it's overwhelming. How are we supposed to fight something like that?"

"With faith," Daniel said simply. "And with each other. None of us can do this alone."

The Great Commission Reaffirmed

Back at NLRM, the team gathered in the prayer room, a small, dimly lit space filled with donated Bibles and handwritten prayer requests pinned to the walls.

Daniel opened his Bible and read from **Matthew 28:18-20**: 'Then Jesus came to them and said, "All authority in heaven and on earth has been given to me. Therefore, go and make disciples of all nations, baptizing them in the name of the Father and of the Son and of the Holy Spirit, and teaching them to obey everything I have commanded you. And surely, I am with you always, to the very end of the age."'

He closed the Bible and looked around at the group. "This is our mission. It's not just about handing out literature or saying the right words. It's about living the truth, showing people the light in a world full of darkness."

David felt a weight lift off his shoulders as he absorbed the words. For the first time, he didn't feel alone in his struggles. He looked around at the group—Eddy, Loyd, Jason, Tree, and Daniel—and felt a sense of unity he hadn't experienced in years.

A New Resolve

As the group dispersed, David stayed behind, lingering in the quiet of the prayer room. He knelt by one of the benches, his hands clasped tightly. "God," he whispered, "I don't know if I'm strong enough for this. But if this is what you want from me, I'll try. Just... don't let me fail."

Unbeknownst to David, Daniel stood silently at the door, a faint smile on his face. He had seen many men walk through the doors of NLRM, but there was something different about David. Something destined.

FORESHADOWING

Later that night, as David lay in his bunk, he couldn't shake the feeling that the fight earlier was just the beginning. He thought of the men in the alley, the darkness in their eyes, and the words Daniel had spoken.

Somewhere, in the depths of his heart, a fire began to ignite—a fire that would prepare him for the battles to come, both seen and unseen.

David drifted into a profound dream of letting go, he dreams of seeds blossoming from the soil, of clearing away the old debris of the past..and in the distance he heard a faint rumble on the horizon and a light growing in his vision, in his soul. And a voice like the rumbling of a waterfall filled his very being, and a sense of overwhelming love and peace washed over him. The voice spoke to him.

The yearning to serve is no accident, you have been chosen to share your light. Step boldly into your role as a luminary, knowing that your courage and faith are not transforming your own life, but the lives of those you touch. Part of your mission, your destiny is to bring light to the world, shine brightly, for the world needs the light only you can bring.

Use your unique experiences to serve others, to lift them up from their own struggles, and inspire them to find their own light.

Your role for now is to guide, inspire, and lead...even though the destination is not yet clear to you. It is the reflection of the Devine spark within you and faith that guide feet, (add the scripture about a voice behind you telling you which way to go).

You are part of the Vanguard a beacon of hope for a world yearning for greater harmony, compassion and spiritual awakening.

PROFOUND DREAMS

David drifted into sleep, a peaceful heaviness overtaking him. His mind opened to a vision unlike any he'd had before. The dream began with a barren garden, dry and lifeless, scattered with debris—broken branches, dead leaves, and stones. Slowly, David knelt in the soil, clearing away the clutter piece by piece. As he worked, the ground beneath him softened, rich and fertile. He planted seeds, and almost immediately, tender shoots broke through the surface, stretching toward the sky.

The horizon shimmered, and in the distance, a faint rumble grew louder, like an approaching storm. But this was no storm—it was a radiant light cresting over the horizon, expanding and enveloping him. The rumble grew into the sound of rushing waters, and the light filled every corner of his being.

A voice, powerful yet gentle, like the rumbling of a waterfall, resonated within him: "The yearning to serve is no accident. You have been chosen to share your light. Step boldly into your role as a luminary, knowing that your courage and faith are not only transforming your life but the lives of all those you touch. You are a beacon, David, uniquely equipped by the fires of your trials to shine in ways no one else can."

The voice continued, each word anchoring itself in David's heart: "Use your experiences—your pain, your joy, your resilience—to lift others from their struggles, to inspire them to discover their own light. Your role is not merely to heal yourself, but to guide, inspire, and lead. Though the destination is veiled, faith will guide your feet."

David felt a pulse of energy, as though his very soul was aligning with the light.

"You are part of the Vanguard, David—a beacon of hope in a world yearning for harmony, compassion, and spiritual awakening. Shine brightly, for the world needs the light that only you can bring. 'Whether you turn to the right or to the left, your ears will hear a voice behind you, saying, "This is the way; walk in it"

(Isaiah 30:21).

The garden in the vision transformed. The light from the horizon consumed the barren field, leaving it lush, green, and alive with blossoms of every color. David stood in the center, the light cascading over him, and tears streamed down his face. He felt a love so complete and overwhelming it left him trembling.

AWAKENING

David jolted awake, his heart racing, his skin damp with sweat, though he felt no fear—only a profound peace. He sat up, the memory of the vision vivid and powerful. He whispered to himself, "A Vanguard... the light... my mission."

The following morning, David shared the dream with Daniel. As they sat outside NLRM, the early sun casting long shadows, Daniel listened intently.

"That wasn't just a dream, David," Daniel said, his voice steady. "It was a message. You've been called, and you're beginning to hear Him more clearly."

David nodded. "But how? How do I step into this role? I've barely begun to figure myself out."

Daniel smiled. "You don't need to have all the answers. Faith isn't about seeing the whole path—it's about taking the next step. And God has already equipped you with everything you need."

Their conversation was interrupted by Eddy and Loyd, who approached with a sense of urgency.

"Hey," Eddy said, his tone serious. "We've got a new outreach planned for today. A neighborhood that hasn't seen much hope in a long time. We need all hands-on deck."

David stood; the dream's message fresh in his mind. "Let's go."

The Mission: Sharing the Light

The team loaded boxes of food, Christian literature, and Bibles into a van and headed to the heart of a struggling neighborhood. As they arrived, children played in the streets, their laughter mixing with the distant hum of traffic. Houses with peeling paint lined the block, and the weariness of the residents was palpable.

Loyd, with his broad shoulders and infectious grin, was the first to step out. "Alright, team, let's get to work."

As they handed out food and shared words of encouragement, David saw something shift in the faces of the people. Hope, faint but growing, flickered in their eyes

Confrontation: Forces of Darkness

As they wrapped up, a group of men emerged from an alleyway, their presence heavy with malice. They were no ordinary troublemakers— these were mortal agents of the faction, practitioners of dark arts. One held a small totem, carved and smeared with blood, chanting under his breath.

"You don't belong here," the leader growled, stepping forward. "This is our territory."

Loyd stepped in front of the group, his imposing frame a wall of protection. "We're here to spread light. You can't stop that."

The men attacked. Loyd took on two at once, his strength overpowering their fury. Jason darted around, his small frame making him hard to catch, while Tree used his height and reach to subdue another. David faced the man with the totem, feeling the weight of the spiritual battle pressing against him.

Daniel moved swiftly, his presence almost otherworldly, as if guided by an unseen force. He disarmed one of the attackers with precision and stood by David's side.

"Remember the dream," Daniel whispered.

David felt a surge of faith. He knocked the totem from the man's hand and shouted, "You have no power here!" The man recoiled as if struck, and the darkness seemed to lif Victory and Reflection The attackers fled; their confidence shaken. The group gathered, bruised but victorious. David looked at Daniel. "That wasn't just a fight.

That was a test."

Daniel nodded. "And you passed. Faith isn't just about words, David. It's about action."

As they drove back to NLRM, David stared out the window, the dream echoing in his mind. The light, the garden, the voice—they were all preparing him for something greater.

The journey was just beginning.

The Demonic Realm: A Grand and Diabolical Council

In the depths of the demonic realm, a grand council convened in a towering chamber of blackened obsidian. The air shimmered with malevolent energy, and the room pulsed with the chaotic rhythm of infernal power. Lilith stood at the center of the gathering, her form radiant with dark allure, her eyes burning with an ancient hatred.

The council was not merely a meeting; it was a spectacle of infernal grandeur. Massive columns of twisted bone spiraled toward a ceiling hidden by swirling black smoke. Thrones of tortured souls circled the chamber, each occupied by a high-ranking demon whose appearance defied mortal comprehension—forms shifting between monstrous and grotesquely beautiful.

At the head of the assembly, a towering figure cloaked in shadow presided. It was not Satan himself but a close lieutenant who bore his authority, an archdemon known as Malzathiel. His voice resonated like the grinding of tectonic plates.

"We are weakened," Malzathiel growled, his claws scraping against his throne. "The light-bearers are encroaching on our plans. Denver teeters on the edge of awakening, and we cannot allow that."

Lilith stepped forward, her voice a melodic whisper that cut through the room. "Then we must turn weakness into strength. Give me leave, Malzathiel. I will bring forth an army to crush their hope before it has a chance to take root."

Malzathiel gestured for her to continue.

"I shall perform a ritual—a union of mortal sin and demonic essence. Through this, I will bring forth Nephilim-like creatures, hybrids to infiltrate their ranks and sow chaos among them. They will carry our will into the mortal world, bending it to our design."

Malzathiel's eyes glowed like molten lava. "You have my blessing, Lilith. Fail, and the consequences will be eternal."

Lilith bowed, her smile a wicked promise.

The Mortal Realm: The Satanists' Dark Ritual

In a remote warehouse on the outskirts of Denver, a coven of Satanists gathered. The room was lit by a circle of crimson candles, their flickering light casting grotesque shadows on the walls. At the center of the room was an altar, carved with blasphemous symbols, where Lilith's essence would be summoned.

The leader of the coven, a gaunt man with hollow eyes named Victor, raised a ceremonial dagger, its blade dripping with sacrificial blood. Around him, his followers chanted in a guttural, ancient tongue, their voices blending into a cacophony of unholy devotion.

"Master of the Abyss," Victor intoned, "accept our offering and bless us with your servant Lilith. Through her, may we bring ruin to the light."

The air grew thick, and a sulfuric stench filled the room. The candles' flames turned black as Lilith materialized in a swirl of smoke and ash. Her presence silenced the chanting, her beauty both mesmerizing and terrifying.

Victor fell to his knees. "Mistress Lilith, we are your humble servants. What is your will?"

"Rise," she commanded, her voice like velvet laced with venom. "Prepare the chalice and the bloodstone. The ritual must begin at once."

The coven obeyed, preparing the sacred implements. Lilith ascended the altar, her body glowing with unearthly light as she began the incantation.

The Birth of Darkness

As the ritual reached its climax, the warehouse shook violently. Lilith's form writhed as she absorbed the dark energy coursing through the bloodstone. With a final, piercing scream, her body became engulfed in a crimson glow.

Moments later, she stepped down from the altar, her abdomen visibly swollen. "The seed is planted," she announced, her voice triumphant. "From my womb will come soldiers of the abyss, half-mortal, half-demonic, bound to our cause."

Victor and his followers cheered; their devotion renewed.

The Plan: Poisoning Denver's Awakening

Lilith turned her attention to the coven. "You have done well, but our mission is far from over. To ensure the success of our forces, we must blind Denver to the light."

Victor stepped forward, his face alight with zeal. "We have the means, Mistress. We've acquired fluoride to taint the water system. And our chemists are ready to disperse aluminum oxide through the air, seeding despair and confusion. The pineal glands of the faithful will calcify, cutting them off from spiritual awakening."

Lilith smiled, her teeth gleaming like daggers. "Excellent. Execute the plan without delay. We will make Denver a stronghold of darkness, a city where hope dares not tread."

The coven dispersed; each member driven by their unholy mission. Lilith remained, her hand resting on her swelling stomach, her smile one of dark anticipation.

A Glimmer of Hope

As the satanists plotted, the forces of light stirred. Unseen by the coven, a single dove perched outside the warehouse, its eyes glowing faintly with divine light. It took flight, carrying the news to unseen allies, a sign that the battle for Denver was far from over.

The stage was set. The lines between light and darkness were drawn, and the struggle for the soul of a city was about to reach its zenith.

The Call of the Night

Every night, David's dreams deepened in intensity. They were not the fleeting images of a wandering mind but vivid, symbolic visions charged with divine meaning. These dreams seemed to beckon him toward an awakening, yet their meanings often lingered just out of reach.

Between these altered states, David would rise, the pull of the night air undeniable. As if summoned, he would step outside, the stillness of the world providing a canvas for his communion with the divine. He would find a quiet place, often in a patch of grass kissed by moonlight, and fall to his knees in prayer.

This nightly ritual mirrored that of Jesus, who also sought solace in solitary prayer under the stars: "Very early in the morning, while it was still dark, Jesus got up, left the house, and went off to a solitary place, where He prayed" (Mark 1:35).

David would sit in silence, opening his heart and mind to the whisper of God, reflecting on his purpose and the dreams that seemed to guide him.

A Sacred Portal

These dreams became a sacred portal, where the veil separating the material and spiritual realms thinned. In these moments, David experienced clarity that transcended logic, as if glimpsing the mind of God. As he reflected, the words of Psalm 23:3 resonated in his soul: "He restores my soul; He guides me along the right paths for His name's sake."

THE DREAMS

1. The Phoenix and the Abyss

In one dream, David stood at the edge of a vast, bottomless chasm. The air was heavy with despair, and voices of anguish echoed from the abyss. Yet, from the darkness emerged a phoenix, its wings ablaze with golden light. It flew toward David, and with each beat of its wings, the cries of despair transformed into a celestial chorus. The phoenix spoke without words: "From the ashes of your trials, you shall rise, bearing the light of hope."

The chasm began to fill with water, creating a tranquil sea. David understood this to mean that the sorrows of the past could be healed, their depth replaced with peace and purpose.

2. The Tree of Life

In another dream, David found himself in a lush garden, at the center of which stood a massive tree whose roots glowed like molten gold. The branches bore fruit that shimmered with an otherworldly light, and each fruit seemed to hold a universe within it. A voice spoke from the tree: "You are a branch of this tree, David.

Your trials have pruned you, and now you will bear fruit for the world to taste and see that I am good."

David reached for a fruit, and as he bit into it, visions of people from his past flashed before him—those he had hurt, those who had hurt him, and those he had saved. He awoke with tears streaming down his face, a renewed determination to bring healing to others.

3. The Labyrinth of Light and Shadow

One night, David dreamed he was walking through an endless labyrinth. On one side, the walls were bathed in radiant light, and on the other, they were cloaked in shadow. As he walked, shadowy figures reached for him, whispering lies and doubts.

But each time David felt himself faltering, he heard a voice behind him, gentle yet firm, saying: "This is the way; walk in it" (Isaiah 30:21). The light walls began to pulse with life, and vines of pure light extended, pulling him forward. When David reached the labyrinth's center, he found a glowing mirror.

Looking into it, he saw not his reflection but a vision of himself as a guide, leading others out of the labyrinth of their own darkness.

4. The River of Souls

In one of the most profound dreams, David stood on the bank of a river. The water shimmered with the faces of countless souls, some crying out for help, others singing in praise. A voice thundered like a waterfall: "You are called to guide these souls to the living water. Shine brightly, for the world needs the light only you can bring."

The river began to part, revealing a path of golden light leading toward a radiant city on the horizon. David knew this city represented God's kingdom and that his journey was to guide others toward it.

Awakening

Each morning, David awoke from these dreams not with fear or confusion but with an overwhelming sense of peace and purpose. He understood that these visions were not merely dreams but divine messages shaping his mission.

The clarity he gained through these nights of prayer and dreaming forged a stronger resolve within him. David began sharing his experiences with those around him, inspiring them to reflect on their own spiritual journeys.

And so, as David walked this path of faith, his dreams became his compass, guiding him through the labyrinth of life and toward the destiny God had prepared for him—a destiny not just for his own redemption but for the awakening of those whose lives he touched.

Visions in the Night and Bonds Forged by Grace

David's dreams had evolved into something far beyond the hazy, fleeting images most people forget upon waking. Each night, as he closed his eyes, the veil between realms seemed to lift, revealing vibrant, other-worldly landscapes. In one dream, David stood at the edge of a vast garden—lush and wild, yet encumbered by a tangled mess of thorny vines and broken branches. A golden light illuminated the garden, urging him to act.

A voice, deep as a waterfall yet soothing as a summer breeze, echoed through his mind: "David, this is your heart, your soul. Tend to it. Clear away the debris of doubt, pain, and betrayal, so the seeds of purpose I have planted may grow. Let go of the past—not to forget, but to create."

As David began pulling away the brambles, new life emerged beneath his touch. Trees unfurled their leaves toward the light, and flowers blossomed with hues he had no words to describe. In the distance, the golden light expanded, pulsing like a heartbeat, as the faint silhouette of a figure approached.

David jolted awake, heart pounding. The dream lingered, its meaning clear but unsettling in its implications. Rising from his bed, he felt the irresistible pull to step outside. The night was still, the stars casting their silent gaze across the world. David wandered to a secluded patch of grass behind the Rescue Mission, knelt, and prayed.

"Lord, guide me. My life has been a storm, but I feel your peace calling me. Teach me to let go, to trust your plan."

The stillness of the moment brought to mind the words of Psalm 23:3: "He restores my soul; He guides me in the paths of righteousness for His name's sake."

David remained there, breathing in the crisp air, letting it carry away the burdens of his soul.

The next day, Eddy noticed something different about David—an energy, a light in his eyes. Sitting down together at breakfast, Eddy shared his story.

"You know," Eddy began, his voice carrying the weight of years gone by, "when I first came to Denver, I was as lost as you felt when I found you. My life wasn't always about faith. I was running from something... or maybe from everything. It took a lot of hard lessons, a lot of failure, to hear God calling me."

David listened intently as Eddy described the hardships that shaped him—growing up in a home that felt like a battleground, losing friends to violence, and finally hitting rock bottom in the depths of addiction.

"But God," Eddy said, his face lighting up, "He doesn't waste anything. Every scar, every regret—it all led me to this place, to this mission. And now, I see it. I see why He had me go through it all—so I could help guys like you."

David's thoughts returned to his dream and to the brambles he had pulled away. "Eddy... do you think it's possible to let go of something you've carried for so long, you don't even know who you are without it?"

Eddy smiled. "Letting go isn't forgetting, brother. It's about creation. It's about making room for what God wants to do with you. And trust me—He's not done with you yet."

Interlude: Prophetic Dreams

That night, David dreamed again. This time, he found himself standing atop a mountain, staring down into a churning sea of darkness. Shadowy forms writhed below, their voices a cacophony of despair.

A beam of light pierced the Chaos, revealing a path that wound through the shadows. The voice returned: "The way is narrow, but I am with you. Step boldly into the light."

As David took his first step, the darkness recoiled, hissing like a wounded serpent. The light enveloped him, lifting him above the turmoil. In the distance, he saw others walking their own paths, their lights shining like beacons.

One of those lights grew brighter, resolving into a figure David recognized—Daniel. Clad in radiant armor, Daniel stood firm, his sword raised high. Behind him, a host of warriors emerged, their presence radiating power and peace.

David awoke, breathless but filled with purpose.

Connecting the Threads

The dream's clarity left David with a profound realization: this wasn't just about him. The people in his life—Daniel, Eddy, Loyd, and the others—were part of a much larger plan. As he shared his vision with Daniel, the older man nodded knowingly.

"You're not walking this path alone, David," Daniel said. "We're all chosen to play a part. Trust the process, even when the destination isn't clear."

David's resolve deepened. The trials of his past, the struggles he still faced—none of it was wasted. And as the sun rose over Denver, he knew he wasn't just following the light. He was becoming it.

Bonds of Flesh and Shadow

The ritual chamber was dimly lit by the flicker of crimson candles, their shadows writhing against the walls like living entities. A heavy, acrid scent filled the air—a mix of burning herbs, sulfur, and metallic tang. The satanists had gathered in secret, cloaked in dark robes, their hoods obscuring their faces. Their leader, a gaunt man with hollow eyes and a cruel smile, stood at the altar, a twisted symbol carved deep into its blackened surface.

Before him knelt Lilith, her beauty both otherworldly and unnerving. Her eyes glowed with an amber hue that seemed to pierce through the veils of mortality. The satanists chanted in guttural tones, a language ancient and vile, their voices rising in a crescendo as the ritual reached its climax.

The leader raised a ceremonial dagger, its blade forged of obsidian and etched with runes. "Mistress of Night, we summon you to give us strength! To birth a new legion that will strike fear into the hearts of men!"

Lilith's lips curled into a smile, both seductive and sinister. She stood, her flowing gown parting to reveal her alabaster skin, marred only by faint, glowing sigils that began to pulse with light. "You call for a legion?" she purred. "Then let it be so. But know this—what you ask comes with a price."

The leader faltered for a moment, his hands trembling. "We... we are prepared to pay it."

Lilith's laughter was low and cold. She stepped toward the altar and laid herself upon it, her arms stretched wide as if in surrender. The room filled with an oppressive heat as dark energy began to swirl around her, forming tendrils of Shadow that snaked across her body. The air itself seemed to vibrate as the satanists' chants reached a fever pitch.

From the darkness, something emerged—a grotesque, clawed hand reaching out to touch Lilith's abdomen. She convulsed, her body arching as a blinding light burst forth. The shadows coalesced into her womb, and with it, the seed of their master took root.

Moments later, the room fell silent. The satanists stared in awe as Lilith rose, her figure now swollen with an unnatural pregnancy. Her eyes burned brighter, and her voice rang out like a chorus of demons. "You shall have your army. But beware—they will obey only me."

Transition to the Heavenly Realms

Above the mortal plane, the dove soared higher, its wings gleaming with radiant light. It ascended through layers of reality, breaking through the clouds and into a realm of pure, unblemished light.

The heavenly realm was vast, a tapestry of golden hues and ethereal structures that seemed to hum with divine energy. Towering beings of light—seraphim— stood guard, their six wings aflame with holy fire. Their eyes burned with wisdom, and their voices, when raised, could shake the very foundations of creation.

The dove descended onto a grand dais where the Archangel Michael stood, clad in resplendent armor that shimmered like molten gold. His sword, the blade of eternity, was sheathed at his side, it's very presence exuding power.

The seraphim nearest to him turned, their fiery forms flickering with anticipation. One spoke, its voice like a chorus of trumpets. "A message from the mortal plane."

The dove transformed mid-flight, morphing into a luminous being —a messenger angel cloaked in white, its face serene yet urgent. "My lord Michael," it began, "a great evil stir. The fallen one's servants are gathering strength in Denver, and Lilith herself has taken mortal seed. A legion will soon rise."

Michael's expression hardened, his hand instinctively resting on the hilt of his sword. "Their audacity knows no bounds," he said, his voice resonating through the realm.

Another seraph, taller than the rest and bathed in azure fire, stepped forward. "Shall we intervene, my lord? The mortals must not face this alone."

Michael raised a hand, his gaze fixed on the horizon where the mortal realm lay veiled. "We will not act hastily. The Vanguard is in place. David, Daniel, and their allies are more important now than ever. But we must prepare."

With a sweep of his wings, Michael turned to the assembly. "Summon the Watchers and the Guardians. If these legion rises, we will meet it head-on."

A Soul in Shadow

The streets of Denver were shrouded in a heavy darkness, one that seemed to linger even during the brightest days. The presence of Lilith's minions had begun to manifest in subtle yet devastating ways. Addiction clinics were overwhelmed, violence was escalating, and whispers of despair were more common than laughter. David and his group had noticed the change, though at first, they didn't fully understand its source.

One evening, as David, Eddy, Daniel, and the others prepared boxes of Christian literature to distribute, David felt an inexplicable heaviness in his chest. He paused mid-motion, holding a pamphlet, and looked out the window toward the city skyline, now dimmed by an unnatural haze.

"There's something out there," he said softly. His voice carried a gravity that caused everyone to stop and listen.

"What do you mean?" Eddy asked, his tone cautious.

David furrowed his brow, as if trying to grasp something just out of reach. "I don't know. It feels... wrong."

Daniel, always perceptive, nodded. "We've felt it too. The attacks aren't just physical. People are losing hope, David. Something is feeding on it."

THE ENCOUNTER

Later that night, the group ventured out to distribute their literature. As they moved through the neighborhoods, they encountered a young man named Victor. His hollow eyes and trembling hands spoke of years lost to addiction, yet there was something in his demeanor that set him apart. He carried a strange aura of conflict, as if waging a battle within himself.

Victor approached David hesitantly. "Are you... the guy who talks about God?"

David smiled gently. "I am, but I don't just talk about Him. I live for Him. What's on your mind?"

Victor glanced around nervously. "I don't know if you can help me. I've done... things."

Eddy stepped closer, his presence reassuring. "Haven't we all? What matters is what you do now."

Victor's voice dropped to a whisper. "I was one of them. I was with... her."

David stiffened. "Her?" Victor nodded. "Lilith. I didn't know who she was at first. She promised us power, control. But then it got dark. Real dark. I couldn't take it anymore, so I left. But they're coming for me."

LILITH'S GRASP

Victor's story was chilling. He described rituals meant to bind mortals to Lilith's will, involving blood sacrifices and promises of wealth and influence. He spoke of the horrors he had witnessed: people losing their humanity, their eyes turning black as their souls were consumed.

"She's building an army," Victor said, his voice trembling. "She wants to crush anything good in this city, starting with you."

The group exchanged uneasy glances. Daniel placed a hand on Victor's shoulder. "You're brave for coming to us. We'll protect you."

Redemption in the Shadows

That night, the group prayed fervently over Victor. He knelt with them, tears streaming down his face as he confessed his sins. David's voice rang out, steady and powerful, as he quoted Psalm 34:18: "The Lord is close to the brokenhearted and saves those who are crushed in spirit."

As Victor's sobs subsided, a sense of peace settled over the room. But David knew this was just the beginning. They had gained an ally, but they had also drawn the enemy's gaze.

LILITH'S WRATH

In the depths of the spiritual realm, Lilith raged. The loss of Victor was not merely an inconvenience; it was an affront to her plans. She summoned her minions, their twisted forms kneeling before her.

"Find him," she hissed. Her voice dripped with malice. "And find those who took him from me. Make them suffer."

TOWARD THE HEAVENLY REALM

As David drifted into an uneasy sleep, the dove once more carried its message to the seraphim. This time, the angelic host gathered in radiant formation. They were powerful beings, their armor gleaming like molten gold, their wings shimmering with the colors of a thousand sunsets.

One seraph, whose voice resonated like thunder, spoke. "The time has come to intervene. The light must pierce the darkness."

The dove bowed its head, its mission complete. The angels prepared to descend, their presence a beacon of hope for David and his group—and a harbinger of doom for their enemies.

LILITH'S WRATH

In her lair, a chamber of obsidian walls pulsating with a dim, red glow, Lilith paced like a caged predator. Her anger radiated like heat waves, causing her demonic attendants to cower. The air was heavy with the stench of sulfur, and the cries of lost souls echoed faintly, a testament to her dominion.

The loss of Victor was more than a setback; it was a fissure in her carefully constructed plans. She stopped abruptly, her eyes glowing like embers as she summoned one of her generals.

"Malrik," she commanded, her voice both seductive and terrifying. "You will retrieve Victor and the mortals who dared to interfere. Show no mercy."

Malrik stepped forward, his towering form wreathed in shadow. His horns curled menacingly, and his voice was a guttural growl. "It will be done, mistress."

But Lilith was not content to leave the task entirely in his hands. She closed her eyes and reached out with her dark essence, her consciousness slithering through the ether like a serpent. She planted seeds of discord and despair in the hearts of Denver's inhabitants, amplifying their fears and weaknesses.

David's Prophetic Dream: A Call to Arms

As Lilith plotted, David was thrust into another prophetic dream. He found himself standing on the edge of a great battlefield, the sky above torn between light and darkness. Angels and demons clashed in a cacophony of sound, their weapons ringing out like thunder.

In the midst of the chaos, a figure emerged—a young woman, her face obscured by shadows. She held out a hand to David, her voice soft but insistent. "You must choose, David. Will you lead the charge, or will you fall with the rest?"

David tried to respond, but the ground beneath him shifted, and he was swallowed by a flood of images: Victor's face, etched with both fear and hope; the city of Denver, its skyline engulfed in flames; and finally, a blinding light, piercing the darkness like a sword.

When he awoke, his body was drenched in sweat, and his heart pounded like a drum. He knew the dream was not just a figment of his imagination but a message —one that demanded action.

The Seraphim Descend: A Divine Intervention

Meanwhile, in the heavenly realms, the seraphim gathered in a circle of radiant fire. Their forms were both beautiful and fearsome, with six wings each—two covering their faces, two covering their feet, and two allowing them to hover effortlessly. Their voices sang in perfect harmony, a song of praise that reverberated through the cosmos.

The leader of the seraphim, whose name was Elyon, stepped forward. His armor was inscribed with celestial runes, and his sword burned with holy fire. "The enemy has overstepped," he declared. "It is time to send a message."

The dove that had carried David's prayers hovered nearby, its white feathers shimmering like polished pearl. It let out a soft coo, as if affirming Elyon's words.

Elyon raised his sword high, and a beam of light shot forth, descending toward the earthly plane. "Let the mortals know they are not alone," he said, his voice echoing like the tolling of a great bell.

Victor's Redemption: A Battle Within

Victor, still recovering from his encounter with David's group, began to feel the pull of his old life. The voices of doubt whispered to him, tempting him to return to the familiar chains of darkness.

But in the quiet moments, when he was alone, Victor found himself drawn to the Bible that Daniel had given him. One passage stood out, as if highlighted by an unseen hand: "I will give you a new heart and put a new spirit in you; I will remove from you your heart of stone and give you a heart of flesh" (Ezekiel 36:26).

As he read, a warmth spread through his chest, pushing back the shadows that had long plagued him. He realized that redemption was not just possible—it was within reach.

A Heavenly Sign

That night, as David and the group prayed, a brilliant light pierced the darkness. It descended from the heavens like a comet, but instead of destruction, it brought peace. The light formed into the shape of a seraph, its wings outstretched, and its voice like the sound of rushing waters.

"Take courage," the seraph said. "You are not alone in this battle. Stand firm, for the Lord is with you."

The group was awestruck, their fears replaced by an unshakable resolve. They knew the road ahead would be fraught with danger, but they also knew they were part of something greater—a divine plan that could not be thwarted.

The Battle Within
Victor

Victor sat alone in the dim light of the small room where Daniel had left him. The Bible rested on the table before him, the passage from Ezekiel replaying in his mind like a melody. "A new heart... a new spirit..." The words offered hope, but they also stirred a conflict deep within him.

He closed his eyes and was transported to an inner battlefield. On one side stood his former self, cloaked in shadows, a figure of greed, lust, and violence. On the other side was a version of himself he barely recognized—a man of peace, light, and purpose.

"Why do you resist?" hissed the shadow self. Its voice was like nails scraping glass. "You've seen what the world does to the weak. The only way to survive is to take."

Victor's other self stepped forward, its voice calm but firm. "That is a lie. True strength comes from love, from surrendering to something greater."

The two figures clashed, their battle spilling into vivid flashes of his past—the lives he had destroyed, the love he had forsaken, the fleeting moments of joy he had, squandered. Each memory was a dagger, cutting deep.

As the battle raged, Victor cried out, "God, if you're real, if you can hear me, I can't do this alone!"

In that instant, the darkness shattered, replaced by a blinding light. Victor fell to his knees, tears streaming down his face. He felt a warmth unlike anything he had ever known, a love so profound it left him trembling.

"You are forgiven," a voice said, resonating from within the light. "Now rise and walk in the light of truth."

The Heavenly Hosts Respond

The seraphim stood ready, their celestial armor gleaming like molten gold. Each bore a sword of light, inscribed with divine runes that pulsed with power. Elyon, the leader, spread his six wings and addressed his warriors.

"The enemy moves to corrupt the city and the hearts of its people. But the prayers of the faithful have reached the throne, and the Most High has sent us to intervene."

The dove that had carried David's prayer now hovered above Elyon; its white wings radiant. "The time has come to strike at the heart of darkness," Elyon declared.

With a collective cry that shook the heavens, the seraphim descended. Their approach was like a storm of light, piercing the veil between the spiritual and mortal realms.

A Clash in the City

As the group prayed in Denver, the air grew heavy, charged with an unseen energy. David opened his eyes to see a dark mist swirling at the edge of the park.

From the shadows emerged demonic forms—twisted, humanoid figures with glowing red eyes and jagged claws.

"Stay strong," David said, standing and lifting his arms. "We are not alone."

Suddenly, the seraphim appeared, their arrival marked by a burst of light that sent the demons reeling. Elyon stepped forward; his sword raised high. "Depart, foul creatures, for you tread on sacred ground!"

The demons hissed and lunged, but the seraphim met them with divine might. Elyon's sword cut through darkness like a beacon, each strike accompanied by a burst of radiant energy.

Big Loyd, inspired by the celestial warriors, grabbed a fallen tree branch and swung it with all his strength, knocking two demons aside. Tree used his towering height to shield the smaller members of the group, while the resourceful man darted between the shadows, distracting the enemy.

David felt a surge of courage and began to pray aloud, his voice steady and commanding. The words seemed to amplify the light around him, forcing the demons to retreat.

A Sign of Victory

As the battle ended, a glowing symbol appeared in the sky—a cross surrounded by a circle of flame. The seraphim bowed their heads, their voices rising in a harmonious hymn of victory.

Elyon approached David, his fiery eyes softening. "The Lord has chosen you for this battle, David. Do not falter, for your faith is a weapon no darkness can withstand."

David nodded, the weight of his purpose settling on him like a mantle. He looked at his friends, their faces illuminated by the fading light of the seraphim. "This is just the beginning," he said. "We have work to do."

Victor's Redemption Journey

Victor left the small room feeling lighter, but he knew his journey was just beginning. Daniel, sensing the transformation within him, embraced him with a brotherly warmth.

"You've taken the first step," Daniel said. "Now, you must learn to walk in the Spirit. It won't be easy, but you're not alone."

The group welcomed Victor, some with cautious smiles, others with open arms. David approached him, extending his hand.

"We've all been broken," David said. "But that's where God's light shines brightest."

Victor nodded, his voice low. "I don't deserve this. After everything I've done..."

"None of us do," David replied. "That's what makes it grace."

Victor began joining the group in prayer and study, though the shadows of his past still haunted him. During one of their gatherings, he shared a vision he'd had— a city on fire, its people crying out for help, and a figure standing in the midst of the chaos, holding a shield of light.

"I think it's Denver," he said. "And I think God wants me to stand in that fire." David nodded, recognizing the call for what it was. "We'll stand with you."

The Aftermath of the Battle

As the group regrouped, the park felt strangely serene. The demonic mist had dissipated, and the oppressive weight in the air was gone. The seraphim, though no longer visible, left an undeniable imprint on the hearts of those who had witnessed them.

Big Loyd looked at the sky, his gruff voice softening. "I never thought I'd live to see angels."

Tree, always pragmatic, shook his head in disbelief. "This changes everything."

David gathered the group, his face resolute. "What we've seen tonight is proof that this battle isn't just ours. We're part of something much bigger. But it also means the enemy won't stop coming. We have to be ready."

They spent the next few days fortifying their faith, praying together, and reaching out to others in the city. News of their encounter spread, drawing more people to their cause. Victor, though new to the faith, became a pillar of strength, his raw honesty and fervent prayers inspiring others to seek redemption.

A New Threat

Unbeknownst to the group, the forces of darkness were regrouping. Lilith, having recovered from her earlier defeat, stood in a cavernous hall, her eyes blazing with fury. Before her knelt a gathering of demonic figures and their human counterparts, the remnants of the satanic cult.

"We have been weakened," Lilith said, her voice echoing like thunder. "But we are not defeated. The mortals think they have won, but they underestimate our resolve."

She turned to a high-ranking cultist, a man known only as Magnus. "You will lead the next phase. The water supply, the chemtrails—make sure they are implemented without delay."

Magnus bowed. "It will be done, my queen."

Lilith smirked. "And as for the believers... leave them to me."

A Prophetic Dream

That night, David had another dream. He stood on a mountaintop, overlooking Denver. The city was covered in a thick fog, and shadowy figures moved within it. A voice spoke, powerful yet gentle.

"The enemy's plans are unfolding, but take heart. For every step they take in darkness, my light will shine brighter."

David saw a vision of himself and his group standing in the city, holding torches that cut through the fog. Around them, others gathered, their torches igniting one by one.

"Raise your torch," the voice commanded. "And lead my people to safety."

David awoke with a start, the words still ringing in his ears. He shared the dream with the group, and they agreed it was a call to action.

The Call to Action

The group decided to take their mission to the streets of Denver. They started hosting prayer vigils, speaking at community centers, and distributing water and food to the homeless. Their efforts caught the attention of local media, and soon, more people joined their cause.

Victor, in particular, found his calling in outreach. He spoke with passion and conviction, sharing his testimony and encouraging others to seek the light.

But as their influence grew, so did the resistance. Strange incidents began to occur—vehicles sabotaged, supplies stolen, and members of the group threatened.

David knew they were being targeted, but he refused to back down. "This isn't just a battle for Denver," he said. "It's a battle for souls."

The Faction's headquarters, nestled deep in a labyrinth of underground caverns, bustled with activity. Braziers burned with unnatural flames—green and violet— casting ghastly shadows across the jagged walls. The air thrummed with dark energy as the leaders of the Faction gathered in their sanctum, a chamber carved from volcanic stone, its centerpiece a massive altar etched with ancient symbols of chaos and destruction.

A Convergence of Malice

At the head of the gathering was Mortavius, a mortal mastermind of the Faction who wore a crown of bone. His piercing gaze swept the room as he addressed his followers. "We have suffered setbacks. The chosen ones have rallied, and the celestial forces stir. But this is merely a delay, not defeat." His voice was cold, commanding, and devoid of doubt.

Beside him stood Lilith, her presence commanding yet unsettling. Her beauty was otherworldly, her eyes glinting with a malevolent light. Her very aura exuded power and seduction, a reminder that she was no mere servant of darkness but a queen among demons. The swelling of her abdomen was unmistakable now— evidence of the ritual that had taken place weeks prior. She carried within her the spawn of both mortal and demonic essence, an army of hybrids that would soon walk the earth.

"Our numbers are replenishing," she said, her voice a hypnotic melody. "When my children rise, they will be unstoppable. Each of them a perfect blend of human cunning and demonic fury."

Mortavius nodded, gesturing to a large map of Denver spread across a stone table. Markings littered the map, each symbol representing a point of attack. "The fluoride in the water supply will keep their minds dull, their spirits shackled. The aluminum oxide in the chemtrails will calcify their pineal glands, cutting them off

from divine inspiration. And then, when the city is ripe for harvest, we unleash the hybrids."

The Ritual of Desecration

The next phase of their plan required the darkest of magics. A group of satanic cultists, led by a high priestess named Isolde, prepared for the Ritual of Desecration. This ceremony would call forth a powerful demonic entity to ensure their plans succeeded.

In a secluded forest clearing under a blood-red moon, the cultists gathered. Their chants echoed into the night; a blend of ancient languages long forgotten by the world of men. A goat was sacrificed, its blood collected in an obsidian chalice. Totems carved from bone and adorned with human hair were placed in a precise circle, each representing a different aspect of their dark deity.

As Isolde raised the chalice, the flames in the surrounding torches turned black. A piercing scream erupted from the center of the circle as the ground cracked open, releasing a sulfurous stench. From the chasm emerged a shadowy figure with burning red eyes—a demonic envoy sent to oversee their efforts.

"We serve willingly, oh Lord of the Abyss," Isolde intoned, her voice quivering with a mix of fear and devotion. "Grant us your power to strike down the chosen ones and spread your dominion."

The figure's voice was like grinding stone. "The chosen ones are protected by the Light, but their faith is fragile. Strike at their hearts, sow doubt and despair. And when their spirits falter, deliver the final blow."

A Plan to Break the Faithful

The Faction's leaders knew that physical warfare alone would not be enough. They devised psychological and spiritual attacks, aimed at undermining the faith of the chosen ones. Each hybrid child, once born, would be assigned a specific target—a chosen one or their allies. They would infiltrate their lives, posing as friends, lovers, or confidants, whispering lies and manipulating them into betrayal.

Lilith herself would lead this charge, using her unparalleled ability to manipulate human desire. "Faith is their shield," she said, her tone mocking. "But faith can be eroded. We will tempt them, isolate them, and make them doubt the very purpose they fight for."

A Gathering Storm

As the plans unfolded, David began to feel a heaviness in his spirit during his dreams. Shadows clawed at the edges of his visions, and the warmth of the Light seemed harder to grasp. The forces of good sensed the growing darkness, and the dove has reached the celestial realms.

In the heavenly realms, where the dove reaches a council of seraphim. Their radiant forms, each unique, pulsated with divine energy. These were beings of incomprehensible power, their six wings adorned with shimmering feathers that refracted light into cascading rainbows. Their voices were like choirs, harmonizing in a language that resonated with creation itself.

As the dove delivered its message, one of the seraphim, named Zephariel, rose. "The darkness moves swiftly. We must prepare the chosen ones for the trials ahead."

Another seraph, Cassiel, whose wings bore the stars of the cosmos, replied, "Their faith wavers. If they fall, the balance will tip. We must intervene."

Zephariel turned to an orb of light hovering in the center of the council chamber. "Send a vision to Daniel. He must guide David and the others to strengthen their resolve. And prepare the Vanguard. The time for passive protection has passed."

A ARON B ELLERI

The Celestial Council

The heavenly chamber resonated with the combined power of the seraphim as they deliberated on their strategy. In the center of the luminous space, the orb of light began to expand, projecting a vision of Earth. It revealed the intricate web of darkness spreading from Denver like a cancer, and the hybrids being bred to infiltrate and corrupt the chosen ones.

Zephariel, whose wings shimmered with pure gold, spoke first. "The hybrids are not bound by the natural laws of humanity. They will strike at the hearts of our chosen and weave themselves into their lives. Their power lies in subtlety and deception, and once their roots are planted, they will be difficult to extract."

Cassiel, the Watcher of Souls, gazed into the orb. His eyes reflected endless galaxies, symbolizing his dominion over divine insight. "Their tactics mirror the snake in Eden, whispering half-truths and false promises. David and his allies must not only resist but grow stronger through these trials. Let the light shine brighter in their struggle."

Another seraph, Taliael, the Guardian of Dreams, stepped forward. Her presence radiated serenity, her wings a cascade of silver and blue. "I will guide their visions. Let their dreams become both warning and weapon, awakening the strength within them."

Zephariel nodded. "And I will send forth the Vanguard. The hybrids will not expect us to strike first."

The Heavenly Vanguard

In a hall adjacent to the council chamber, rows of celestial warriors—angels who bore the marks of battle—stood ready. Their armor gleamed with a brilliance that no darkness could tarnish. Each carried a weapon forged from divine energy, pulsing with the essence of creation. These were the Vanguard, warriors of the highest order tasked with direct intervention when the stakes demanded it.

Zephariel entered the hall, his golden presence commanding silence. "Brothers and sisters, the time has come. The Faction seeks to extinguish the Light in this world. But we will not stand idle. While the chosen ones grow in strength, we will cut down the hybrids before they reach their full power."

The Vanguard raised their weapons in unison, their voices a chorus of resolve. Zephariel continued, "Their sanctuaries are hidden, but the Light sees all. Follow my lead. Let no shadow escape."

As they prepared to descend, the seraphim sent a blessing over the Vanguard. Each angel's weapon flared brighter, resonating with the collective will of Heaven.

The Faction's Preparations

Back in the cavernous sanctum of the Faction, Mortavius and Lilith strategized their next moves. The hybrids were being nurtured in pods that pulsed with a sickly green glow, fed by a mixture of demonic essence and stolen human vitality. The chamber housing them was like a grotesque hive, its walls lined with veined, fleshy sacs.

Mortavius paced before the pods, his sharp mind racing. "The hybrids will not only infiltrate their ranks but also sow chaos among the unchosen. Riots, despair, and division—they will destabilize everything, making it impossible for the chosen ones to rally."

Lilith ran her hand over one of the pulsating pods. "Their human hearts will make them perfect instruments of manipulation, while their demonic nature ensures loyalty to the cause."

A cultist entered the room, bowing deeply. "My queen, the preparations for the next ritual are complete. We will harness the ley lines beneath the city to amplify our power."

Lilith smiled, a sinister gleam in her eyes. "Excellent. The hybrids will march, and the world will tremble."

David's Awakening

As the seraphim prepared their forces, David's dreams intensified. One night, he saw himself standing in a wasteland, surrounded by twisted, shadowy figures. At the center of the desolation was a massive, glowing fissure in the earth. From its depths rose Lilith, her hybrid army behind her. Their eyes burned with malice, and David could feel the weight of their hatred bearing down on him.

But then a voice spoke, cutting through the darkness like a blade of light. "Do not fear, David. The battle is not yours alone."

Turning, he saw Taliael, her silver wings enveloping him. She handed him a sword that radiated divine energy. "You are chosen to lead, but you are not alone.

Others will come to your side, drawn by the same Light that guides you. Trust in the path, even when it seems uncertain."

David woke with a start, the weight of the dream pressing on his chest. But he also felt something new: a spark of hope. He knelt by his bed, praying for clarity, as the Light began to strengthen within him.

The Shadows of Dominion

Deep in the bowels of a forgotten cathedral, far from prying eyes and sanctified grounds, the Faction convened. The ruins, desecrated long ago, had become their haven, where dark rites shaped the destiny of mortal and immortal alike. The towering altar, constructed of black obsidian and etched with ancient symbols, pulsed with an unnatural light. Around it, the high priests of the Faction murmured incantations in a guttural language older than human speech, summoning forth the ancient spirit of Lilith.

Lilith's presence was commanding, her form both terrifying and alluring. Draped in a gown of shadows, she moved like smoke, her voice carrying both venom and seduction. The priests knelt before her, presenting her with offerings: blood-filled chalices, ancient relics, and the bound souls of those foolish enough to cross the Faction.

"You summon me to birth your army," Lilith hissed, her voice echoing like nails across glass. "Do you understand the price?"

The lead priest, a man with piercing black eyes and a voice heavy with arrogance, spoke. "We offer our very essence to strengthen your seed. The hybrids will rise—half human, half infernal. They will walk among mortals, unseen but not unfelt. They will poison the hearts of men and sow chaos in the Vanguard's path."

Lilith's laughter was both beautiful and horrifying, her form momentarily expanding into a towering shadow that swallowed the room. "Then so be it."

The ritual began. Each priest spilled their blood upon the altar, their vitality drained as they chanted forbidden rites. The air grew thick with sulfur and ash, and the temperature dropped sharply. Lilith, kneeling on the altar, let out an unearthly scream as the dark energy of the ritual infused her being. Her form convulsed, her flesh shifting as the monstrous conception took root. Around her, the air filled with shadowy figures—manifestations of the hybrids waiting to be born.

As Lilith prepared to bring forth the hybrid army, the Faction turned its attention to its grander schemes. The poisoning of Denver's water supply was merely the beginning. A council of human acolytes—master Satanists loyal to the Faction—gathered in a separate chamber beneath the ruins. Maps of Denver sprawled across a blood-stained table, marked with intricate notes and symbols.

"Our mission is clear," the leader announced, a woman with eyes that burned like embers. "The fluoride will dull their minds, but the aluminum oxide will sever their connection to the divine. Without their pineal glands intact, their spiritual awakening will be halted, and their prayers will go unheard."

Another acolyte, a gaunt man with trembling hands, spoke. "And the chemtrails? Will the aerial dispersal be effective?"

The leader sneered. "It already is. The Vanguard is not aware of how pervasive the damage has become. Soon, even their most devout will struggle to hear their God."

One acolyte hesitated. "What of the Vanguard themselves? They have begun to strike at our lesser agents. What if they discover our plans?"

The leader's voice dropped to a venomous whisper. "Let them come. We will be ready. And if they get too close, our hybrids will feast upon their flesh."

MEANWHILE: THE VANGUARD PREPARES

Unbeknownst to the Faction, the Vanguard was not idle. David's dreams had begun to resonate with prophetic clarity. Each vision brought a new piece of the puzzle—a warning about the water, glimpses of shadowy chemtrails, and the haunting image of hybrids tearing through the streets of Denver.

David shared his visions with Daniel, Eddy, and the others. "This isn't just spiritual warfare anymore," David said. "This is a full-scale attack on humanity. If we don't act, they'll destroy Denver before we even have a chance to fight."

Daniel, ever the strategist, suggested a bold move. "We need to gather more than just the Vanguard. If they're poisoning the city, we need to unite the community —the churches, the missions, even those who don't believe yet. We can't do this alone."

Eddy chimed in. "I've got contacts at the mission who can spread the word. But we're going to need more than prayers. We need to counteract whatever they're using."

David nodded; the weight of leadership heavy on his shoulders. "Then we'll fight them on every front. Spiritually, physically, mentally. This is our city, and we won't let them take it."

THE HEAVENLY REALMS MOBILIZE

As David and his allies prepared, the dove sent by the Vanguard ascended into the heavens, reaching the courts of the celestial seraphim. The angels, towering beings of radiant light, were gathered in a chamber that pulsed with divine energy. Each seraph carried a weapon forged from the very essence of heaven—a flaming sword, a radiant spear, a shield that shimmered like a thousand suns.

The dove transformed into a smaller angel, trembling before the seraphim. "The Faction has moved. Lilith prepares her hybrids, and they poison the city of Denver. The Vanguard is strong but outnumbered. They will need reinforcements."

The leader of the seraphim, a being with six wings and eyes of fire, rose. "Then reinforcements they shall have." His voice was a song and a battle cry, shaking the very fabric of reality.

As the seraphim prepared for war, the dove-turned-messenger spoke once more, her voice trembling yet resolute. "For it is written: 'For he will command his angels concerning you to guard you in all your ways' (Psalms 91:11). We must act swiftly, for their faith is strong, and the promise of the Almighty is their shield.

Yet the enemy is relentless, and the stakes have never been higher."

The leader of the seraphim, radian" with divine authority, paused at these words. "Indeed," he said, his fiery eyes fixed on the horizon. "It is our charge to guard them, to ensure that they fulfill their purpose. But the Vanguard must also rise to the occasion. Their faith is a weapon more potent than any blade we carry."

David's Journey

David sat alone under the canopy of stars; his thoughts heavy with the weight of his visions. As he reflected on the battle to come, the words of Psalms 91:11 echoed in his mind, a whisper of reassurance from the divine: "For he will command his angels concerning you to guard you in all your ways."

He closed his eyes and let the words sink into his heart, feeling a surge of hope. Though the path ahead was fraught with danger, David knew he was not alone.

The unseen forces of heaven moved on his behalf, guarding him and his companions as they prepared to face the darkness.

The seraphim prepared for war, their light spreading across the heavens. Beneath them, mortals like David and his companions would soon find their strength bolstered by the unseen hands of heaven.

The Conclave of Shadows

Within the heart of the infernal realm, a council convenes. The air crackles with malice as the demonic generals and their mortal allies discuss their next moves.

Lilith stands at the center, her form pulsating with power, surrounded by her freshly spawned offspring—half-demonic, half-human monstrosities. These creatures are designed for stealth and manipulation, capable of infiltrating society unnoticed while sowing chaos.

Dialogue among the demonic generals reveals: Plans to corrupt sacred institutions, turning places of worship into centers of despair.

A coordinated campaign to flood Denver's air with chemtrails laced with substances that dull spiritual sensitivity.

A plot to contaminate water supplies with compounds that induce despair and apathy in humans, rendering them pliable to dark influences.

Lilith, addressing the council, declares, "The Vanguard is weakening. Their resolve is strong, but their numbers are few. With every corrupted soul, their light dims further. Focus on their young, their hopeful—they are the easiest to twist."

The council erupts in cheers as a ritual begins, summoning an ancient force of chaos to bolster their ranks. Black flames rise, and a guttural chant fills the chamber. Scripture counterpoint: Psalm 91:11—"For he will command his angels concerning you to guard you in all your ways"—serves as a hopeful contrast to the bleakness of this moment.

Transition to the Heavenly Realms The dove, a radiant messenger of hope, has reached the gates of the celestial realm. An angelic host, led by a seraph named Zerachiel, prepares to respond.

Zerachiel's fiery wings and piercing gaze convey both beauty and might. His voice, like thunder rolling through a peaceful valley, commands attention as he gathers the heavenly warriors.

The scene shifts to the assembly of angels as Zerachiel speaks: "We cannot intervene directly, but we can strengthen the hearts of the Vanguard. Let us weave courage into their dreams and wisdom into their actions. The enemy's plans are intricate, but their arrogance blinds them."

The angels spread out, each tasked with inspiring hope, courage, and faith in the hearts of believers. Scripture woven in: Isaiah 30:21—"Whether you turn to the right or to the left, your ears will hear a voice behind you, saying, 'This is the way; walk in it.'"

Back on Earth: The Vanguard's Next Steps

David, Daniel, Eddy, and the others sense a shift. Their prayers grow more fervent, and their resolve strengthens. During one of their nightly gatherings, Daniel shares a vision:

"I saw a garden flourishing under a stormy sky. The seeds of faith are sprouting, but the weeds of doubt and fear threaten to choke them. We must be vigilant, tending to one another's spirits while uprooting despair."

David, emboldened by his own recent dream of stepping into his role as a light-bringer, proposes a bold plan: infiltrate the circles of the lost, not to confront them directly but to plant seeds of doubt within the enemy's ranks. The team agrees, each taking on a specific role to spread hope in unexpected places.

As the Vanguard prepares their next move, a shadow looms near their meeting place. Unbeknownst to them, one of Lilith's hybrid creations has been observing their every step, ready to report back to its dark master.

The Conclave of Shadows

As the demonic council gathers, Lilith's voice rises above the others, laying out her intricate scheme: "Denver must fall—not by force, but through whispers of doubt and subtle rebellion. Its people cling to hope, but hope can be twisted. We shall plant the seeds of apostasy deep within their hearts, starting with those who lead their flocks."

A general named Malphas steps forward, his eyes glowing with dark cunning. "The churches will crumble from within. We'll tempt their leaders with power and greed, turning their focus away from truth and onto worldly gains. Their sermons will lose substance, their prayers, conviction. Soon, their congregations will scatter."

Lilith adds, "And for the wavering, we'll craft new idols. Let them worship the self, the material, and the transient pleasures of this life. We will make them blind to eternity."

As the council deliberates, a sinister plan takes form:

1. Corruption of Clergy: Demons infiltrate the dreams of Denver's spiritual leaders, filling them with visions of personal ambition and success that erode their humility.
2. False Doctrines: Through whispers to influential thinkers,

the enemy introduces subtle heresies—truth mixed with lies —to divide believers.

3. New Age Movements: They encourage movements that promise enlightenment but lead to spiritual dead ends, focusing on human potential over divine guidance.
4. Social Influence: Influencers and media channels are subtly guided to mock faith, glorifying cynicism and self-indulgence.

Lilith concludes, "We will make their faith in God appear outdated and irrelevant. By the time the Vanguard realizes what's happening, it will be too late."

Heavenly Response: Zerachiel's Charge

In the celestial realm, Zerachiel watches the plans unfold. His heart burns with righteous fury, but his wisdom tempers it. Turning to the gathered seraphim, he proclaims, "The enemy sows lies and discord, but we will counter with unity and truth. Denver shall not be lost."

He assigns angels to protect key individuals, strengthening their resolve and filling their hearts with courage. A specific angel, Radiath, is tasked with inspiring a revival among Denver's faithful. Her mission: to plant a yearning for deeper truth that counters the enemy's lies.

Zerachiel also speaks directly to the dove messenger. "Tell the Vanguard this: 'Stay vigilant, for the enemy prowls. Stand firm, for truth will outlast all falsehoods.'"

THE VANGUARD'S GATHERING

David and his companions sense the weight of the battle intensifying. During one of their prayer sessions, Eddy speaks with urgency:

"We've seen the signs—the rise of self-worship, the crumbling of faith in the city. It's happening faster than we thought. This isn't just about us; this is about protecting the light in Denver."

David recalls his dream—a vision of a vibrant garden choked with weeds. He interprets it aloud: "The garden is Denver. The weeds are apostasy, and we're the ones who have to pull them out. But we can't do it alone. We need to rally the faithful and awaken the sleeping."

The group strategizes, deciding to host small gatherings throughout the city to reignite spiritual passion. They distribute materials and share personal testimonies to counter the enemy's influence.

CLIFFHANGER

As David speaks at the first gathering, a figure stands in the shadows—a hybrid creation of Lilith, listening intently, ready to report back to its master.

David sat in the grass under a crescent moon, his heart still and open, as if the universe were holding its breath. He closed his eyes and prayed, seeking guidance, not for himself alone, but for the city and the world now looming larger in his thoughts. Denver had become the frontline of a battle he could scarcely comprehend, and he knew it was time to act.

As he prayed, a new clarity began to emerge, his mind drawn to the faint echoes of the faction's insidious plans—dark whispers that had found their way into his dreams and moments of stillness. He saw their aim clearly now: the apostasy of Denver was not just a spiritual attack but a methodical, deliberate erosion of humanity's connection to the divine.

The Faction's Strategy Revealed

The faction was operating on multiple fronts. Beyond the visible acts of violence and sabotage, they had infiltrated systems critical to Denver's spiritual awakening. David's vision painted a grim picture: planes releasing chemtrails laden with aluminum oxide and fluoride, their purpose sinister—to calcify the pineal glands of the city's inhabitants. The goal was to sever the populace from their natural ability to connect with the divine, to stifle dreams and the whispers of angels.

In the vision, David saw shadowy figures in lab coats working in clandestine facilities, combining scientific precision with dark rituals. Sigils etched into vials of chemicals, blood sacrifices enhancing their potency. Each trail they released was imbued with malevolent intent, designed not just to poison the body but to weigh down the spirit.

Meanwhile, the faction's mortal agents had infiltrated Denver's water treatment plants. By introducing fluoride levels far beyond safety standards, they sought to render the population docile, apathetic, and spiritually blind. David could almost hear their sinister laughter echoing through the machinery.

The Spiritual Counterattack

David awoke with a start, the weight of this knowledge pressing on him like a storm cloud. He knew he couldn't face this alone. Gathering Daniel, Eddy, and the others, he shared what he had seen. Each man bore the burden in silence, the gravity of their mission settling into their hearts. They began planning their next steps—not just to spread the gospel but to confront this evil head-on.

Daniel suggested seeking out others who might have insight into the faction's operations. Eddy, ever resourceful, recalled a small, underground network of Christians who had been exposing similar plots. Among them was a woman named Mary, a fiercely intelligent chemist-turned-activist, who had narrowly escaped the faction's clutches.

A Meeting with Mary

The group arranged to meet Mary in a hidden refuge beneath an old church in Aurora. The place had once been a speakeasy during Prohibition, and now it served as a sanctuary for those fighting against the faction's darkness. Mary greeted them, her eyes sharp but weary.

"I've seen what you're up against," she said, spreading out blueprints of Denver's infrastructure. "They've been targeting areas with high spiritual activity— churches, shelters, even places of natural beauty. Their goal isn't just control; it's corruption."

Mary pointed to a map. "Here, the water treatment plant. Here, the chemtrail distribution center disguised as a private aeronautics firm. And here..." She paused, her finger trembling over a mark labeled Spiritual Nexus.

David leaned closer. "What's at the nexus?"

Mary sighed. "It's Red Rocks Amphitheatre. The natural acoustics there amplify energy, both good and evil. They're planning a massive ritual to desecrate it, to anchor their corruption into the earth itself."

The room fell silent as the weight of her words sank in. The group knew they had to act fast.

A Plan of Action

David proposed a two-pronged approach. Daniel and Eddy would lead a team to gather evidence of the faction's activities, aiming to expose them to the public and rally more support. David, along with Mary and the others, would prepare to confront the spiritual forces directly, reclaiming Red Rocks before it could be defiled.

Mary hesitated. "Do you really believe we can stop them?"

David placed a hand on her shoulder. "We don't fight alone. 'For He will command His angels concerning you to guard you in all your ways.'" (Psalms 91:11).

The words hung in the air, a reminder that their battle was both seen and unseen.

A Rising Threat

Meanwhile, in the depths of the demonic realm, the faction's leaders convened. Lilith, now visibly swollen with her unholy pregnancy, stood at the center of a grand chamber. Shadows twisted and coiled around her as she addressed the assembly.

"Our plans are unfolding," she hissed, her voice both alluring and menacing. "The waters of Denver will flow with our corruption. The skies will carry our despair.

And Red Rocks will be our altar—a gateway to spread our influence across the world."

The gathered demons and mortals cheered, their voices a cacophony of malice. Lilith raised her hands, silencing them.

"But the Vanguard grows stronger," she continued. "David and his allies must be dealt with. I leave it to you to decide how. Fail me, and you will wish for the oblivion you escaped."

As the assembly dissolved, the faction's mortal agents began devising new strategies to counter the Vanguard, unaware that their every step brought them closer to their own undoing.

DAVIDS RESOLVE

Back at the rescue mission, David stood under the stars, his heart both heavy and hopeful. He knew the days ahead would test him in ways he couldn't imagine.

But he also knew this: he wasn't alone.

With faith as his compass and his friends at his side, David was ready to step into the next phase of his journey, knowing that the light within him was more powerful than any darkness.

Strengthening the Vanguard

The Vanguard, realizing the enormity of the faction's plans, begins reaching out to other spiritually gifted individuals. Mary, with her natural empathy, connects with a woman named Esther, a reclusive painter known for creating surreal artworks that eerily predict future events. Esther's latest piece depicts a fiery serpent coiling around Denver, suffocating its light—a clear forewarning of the faction's schemes.

Meanwhile, David and Daniel seek out Joseph, a former soldier turned survivalist who has visions of battles between angels and demons. Joseph is reluctant, haunted by past failures, but a shared vision with David—an ethereal phoenix rising from Denver's ashes—compels him to join.

As they gather, the group trains both physically and spiritually, learning to interpret prophetic dreams, recognize demonic influences, and fortify their faith. This training is crucial, as the enemy's power grows stronger with each passing day.

A Dangerous Mission

The Vanguard learns of a critical meeting at one of the faction's aeronautics facilities. Posing as workers, David, Mary, and Daniel infiltrate the building. The operation is tense; every corner seems to pulse with malevolent energy. They discover blueprints for drones equipped with aerosol canisters, designed to spray chemtrails laced with aluminum oxide.

In the heart of the facility, they find a hidden chamber—a grotesque laboratory where human experiments have taken place. The group narrowly escapes after setting the chamber ablaze, but their victory comes at a cost: Daniel is injured, and they're pursued by shadowy figures long after leaving the facility.

Heavenly Intervention

As the Vanguard regroups, their exhaustion is palpable. David, struggling with self-doubt, steps outside to pray beneath the stars. His prayer is answered in a blaze of light: a seraph descends, its six wings shimmering with celestial fire. The seraphim's voice is both gentle and commanding, its presence overwhelming yet comforting.

The angel reveals that their efforts have drawn the attention of heaven, but the battle ahead will test their resolve like never before. It warns them of a coming trial that will require absolute faith. Quoting Psalms 91:11, the seraphim assures David: "For he shall give his angels charge over thee, to keep thee in all thy ways."

The angel also reveals Esther's next vision—a great battle at Red Rocks Amphitheater, where the faction plans to unleash a ritual that could sever Denver's spiritual connection to the divine. The Vanguard must act swiftly, for the consequences of failure are unthinkable.

Strengthening the Vanguard

As the Vanguard grows, the unity of their group deepens, but so do the challenges. Each member brings unique spiritual gifts but also personal burdens. Mary's past as a healer includes a failure to save her own brother, leaving her hesitant to fully trust her abilities. Joseph, the survivalist, struggles with the idea of spiritual warfare, feeling inadequate to face battles beyond the physical realm. Esther, though a gifted seer, battles overwhelming fear due to the vivid intensity of her prophetic dreams.

David, now stepping into a role of reluctant leadership, begins to forge bonds between them. He encourages Esther to share her visions, despite their unsettling nature. Her next painting captures their attention: a darkened Denver skyline with crimson skies, a single dove in radiant white streaking toward the heavens.

Below, shadowy figures gather at an amphitheater, their forms twisting as if controlled by unseen puppeteers.

The group Interprets this as both a warning and a call to action. As they prepare for what lies ahead, they train not just their bodies but their souls. David initiates nightly prayer gatherings, asking each member to lead in turn. Through these sessions, they discover untapped strength. Mary's hands begin to glow faintly as she prays, an indication of her healing abilities awakening once more. Joseph learns to discern the spiritual nature of his visions, finding courage in the signs of protection surrounding the group.

Uncovering the Faction's Secrets

Through a network of informants, the Vanguard learns that the enemy has doubled its efforts after their recent disruption. The faction, now aware of the Vanguard's interference, tightens security around its operations. David's dreams provide cryptic clues: images of drones releasing silvery mist over neighborhoods, children crying out in confusion, and streams of water running black.

Acting on these dreams, the group investigates a water treatment plant. Late at night, Esther senses a malevolent presence, and the group encounters a demonic guardian—a monstrous entity guarding a hidden room. In a harrowing battle, Mary uses her healing energy as a weapon, forcing the creature to retreat into the shadows. Inside the room, they find blueprints and documents confirming plans to poison Denver's water supply with fluoride compounds designed to calcify the pineal gland, a gateway to spiritual clarity.

Additionally, they uncover plans to utilize chemtrails laden with aluminum oxide. These are designed not only to disrupt health but also to weaken spiritual perception, cutting Denver off from divine influence. The Vanguard realizes the scope of the faction's ambition: to create a city enslaved by spiritual blindness, fertile ground for their demonic master's dominion.

Revelation of the Enemy's Weapon

Returning to their base, the group pores over the stolen documents. One name stands out: Project Black Veil. This secret operation is revealed to be the faction's ultimate weapon—a convergence of ritual magic and technology aimed at creating a "spiritual blackout" over Denver. David experiences a vision of Red Rocks Amphitheater engulfed in flames, with dark tendrils spreading across the city.

Joseph speculates that the amphitheater's unique acoustics and natural formation make it a potent site for the ritual, amplifying the faction's dark energy. Esther's visions confirm this: a shadowy figure—Lilith herself—stands at the center of a massive ritual, drawing power from the sacrifices of her followers.

The Seraphim's Return

As David struggles with the gravity of their mission, the seraphim reappear, its light filling their refuge. Its words are both a warning and a guide: "The forces of darkness know of your presence and will stop at nothing to silence you. But fear not, for the Most High is with you. Strengthen your faith, for it will be your shield. Psalms 91:11 will guide your steps."

The angel reveals that their mission is not merely to stop the ritual but to reclaim Denver as a city of light. The seraphim calls upon them to awaken the latent spiritual power within themselves and their city, encouraging them to seek out Denver's faithful and rally them to prayer.

The group takes this to heart, organizing a clandestine movement among Denver's spiritual communities. They meet with pastors, rabbis, and imams, sharing their knowledge and calling for united intercession. Slowly, the city begins to stir with spiritual activity, a counterforce to the enemy's plans.

The Build-Up to Red Rocks

The enemy senses the Vanguard's movements and begins accelerating their timeline. Lilith's presence grows stronger, her influence spreading across Denver's skies like a storm cloud. The Vanguard, now fully committed, makes their way to Red Rocks, knowing it is the heart of the enemy's plan.

The amphitheater is guarded not just by human acolytes but by demonic entities cloaked in shadow. The group must navigate this treacherous ground, their faith and training put to the ultimate test. Esther paints one final vision before the battle: a blazing cross descending into Red Rocks, piercing the darkness with divine light.

Lilith's Preparations at Red Rocks

As the faction moves closer to the culmination of their plans, Red Rocks Amphitheater becomes a sinister hub of activity. Under the guise of a private "music festival," workers are seen installing large, nondescript equipment in the venue. The machinery, hidden beneath decorative covers, is a network of sound and vibration emitters meant to amplify the occult ritual's reach. These devices have been infused with dark energy through rites conducted by Lilith's most devout followers.

Lilith herself manifests at the amphitheater under a guise of human beauty, directing her acolytes with chilling precision. Her influence causes subtle disturbances in the area—birds avoid the skies above, and hikers report feelings of unease or sudden exhaustion near the site.

A massive, glowing sigil is carved into the stone beneath the amphitheater's stage, visible only to those attuned to spiritual energies. This sigil serves as the ritual's anchor, connecting Red Rocks to the spiritual realm and acting as a conduit for Lilith's power.

The final piece of the faction's preparation involves gathering a congregation of the spiritually lost—those already bound by addiction, despair, or greed. These individuals are to serve as the sacrifice needed to fuel the blackout.

The Vanguard's Infiltration

Meanwhile, the Vanguard prepares to infiltrate Red Rocks. Knowing the enemy expects them, David and the group develop a multi-pronged plan.

1. The Frontline Diversion

Joseph and Esther lead a small group of allies to the amphitheater's main entrance. Disguised as festival attendees, they aim to distract and disrupt the acolytes guarding the perimeter. Esther, carrying a concealed talisman blessed by the seraphim, uses her seer's abilities to identify weak points in the enemy's defenses.

2. The Stealth Team

David, Mary, and a few others take a more covert route through the surrounding wilderness. Navigating hidden trails, they rely on Joseph's survival expertise and Mary's growing sensitivity to demonic presences to avoid detection.

3. Heavenly Assistance

Before the mission, the seraphim promises that divine reinforcements will be watching over them. The group recites Psalms 91:11 as they embark, drawing strength from its promise: "For he will command his angels concerning you to guard you in all your ways."

As the Vanguard approaches, David's sensitivity to spiritual energy increases, allowing him to detect the subtle movements of dark forces within Red Rocks. He sees faint traces of light emanating from their talisman, guiding their steps like a beacon of hope in the oppressive darkness.

Unveiling the Ritual

Inside Red Rocks, the Vanguard discovers the full scope of the ritual. The amphitheater, with its natural acoustics and alignment with spiritual ley lines, has been transformed into a massive altar. The dark sigil beneath the stage pulsates with energy, synchronized with the low hum of the hidden emitters.

Lilith stands at the center of the sigil, her voice weaving an incantation that causes the air itself to shimmer. As the ritual progresses, tendrils of shadow stretch from the sigil, reaching out to the crowd of sacrifices.

David and Mary feel the crushing weight of Lilith's presence, a suffocating aura of despair that threatens to break their resolve. Yet, in that moment, David recalls Esther's vision of the blazing cross. He realizes the only way to counteract the ritual is to invoke divine power directly into the sigil.

CONFRONTATION WITH LILITH

The air inside the cavern was thick, suffocating with an unnatural heat as David and his allies crept closer to the ritual chamber. The walls shimmered faintly, etched with ancient sigils that pulsed with a dark, rhythmic energy. In the center of the vast chamber stood Lilith, her form both beautiful and horrifying. Her presence commanded the room, her every gesture crackling with power as she chanted in a guttural, otherworldly tongue. Around her, hooded figures knelt in a circle, their voices rising in unison as they fed their strength into the sigil carved into the stone floor.

David motioned for his group to spread out, their plan David motioned for his group to spread out, their plan carefully rehearsed but fraught with peril. The sigil carved into the floor glowed malevolently, pulsating like a beating heart. This was the source of Lilith's power—a nexus binding her influence over the physical realm. David knew breaking it was their only chance, but the sigil was heavily protected, both spiritually and physically.

Lilith's voice thundered, a cacophony of malice that shook the chamber walls. Her attention was fixed on the ritual, but as David and his allies stepped closer, she abruptly stopped. The hooded acolytes fell silent, their chant choking in their throats. Lilith turned, her dark eyes blazing with an otherworldly fire, locking onto David.

"You dare?" she hissed, her voice resonating with centuries of hatred. "You think you can challenge me? Pathetic children of clay."

A wave of dark energy surged from her outstretched hand, striking the group like a tempest. David barely managed to raise his spiritual shield; a shimmering barrier of light fueled by his faith. Around him, his allies countered with prayers and divine incantations, the clash of light and dark filling the chamber with blinding flashes and deafening roars.

David moved toward the sigil, his heart pounding. The spiritual weight in the room was suffocating, but he pressed forward. Lilith's power lashed out again, this time aimed directly at him. He braced himself, reciting Psalm 91:11

Retreat to the Mountains

Exhausted and battered, David and his allies made their way into the mountain wilderness, guided by the fading glow of the Seraphim's presence. The terrain was rugged, offering natural concealment, but the journey taxed their weary bodies. Each step felt heavier than the last, the weight of their mission pressing down on them.

They found refuge in a secluded valley surrounded by towering peaks. Here, the Seraphim performed a cloaking ritual, shielding them from demonic detection. A supernatural peace blanketed the area, providing respite from the chaos they had escaped.

For days, the group rested and reflected. The confrontation with Lilith had shaken them all, exposing their vulnerabilities but also forging a deeper bond of trust and purpose. David spent long hours in prayer, seeking guidance for the next steps. It was during one of these moments that a vision came to him.

The Call to the Sleepers

In his vision, David stood on a mountaintop, bathed in golden light. A voice, deep and resonant, echoed in his soul: "Awaken the sleepers. The time of harvest has come. My chosen must gather, for the battle draws near."

David saw flashes of people scattered across the land—ordinary men and women who carried hidden spiritual gifts. They were farmers, teachers, laborers, and wanderers, unaware of their divine purpose. Yet, as the voice called, each one felt a stirring in their hearts, a pull toward the mountains.

When David shared the vision, the group agreed it was a divine mandate. They began sending out spiritual signals—prayers and messages that would guide the sleepers to their location. Slowly, the first of them arrived, drawn by dreams and an inexplicable sense of destiny.

DAVID'S REVELATION

As the numbers grew, the Davidic priesthood—elders who had been waiting for this moment—emerged from the mountains to greet the group. Among them was a scholar who carried an ancient manuscript, preserved through generations.

The manuscript revealed David's true heritage: he was a direct descendant of Shem, the son of Noah, and had been chosen to fulfill the role of Melchizedek, the eternal priest-king.

"You are a priest forever, in the order of Melchizedek," the elder said, quoting Psalm 110:4. "It is your destiny to lead God's army in the final battle against the forces of darkness."

The revelation shook David to his core. He had always felt called but struggled to reconcile his troubled past with such a divine purpose. Now, he realized his hardships had been part of God's preparation, shaping him into the leader he was meant to be.

THE GREAT BATTLE

The dark forces, realizing they had been thwarted, began amassing their army. Demons of every rank and power gathered, their numbers bolstered by fallen mortals who had sworn allegiance to evil. Opposing them, David's army prepared. The Seraphim trained the mortals in spiritual warfare, teaching them to wield faith as a weapon.

The final battle began at dawn, the sky darkened by demonic clouds. Seraphim clashed with towering demons, their swords of light cutting through the darkness.

Mortals stood side by side, chanting prayers and wielding spiritual weapons.

David, at the forefront, radiated a divine light. His voice thundered as he recited scripture, each word striking the enemy like a hammer. Demonic forces crumbled under the weight of God's power, but the battle was far from won.

Lilith, having broken free, appeared on the battlefield, her rage shaking the earth. She charged toward David, her power amplified by the sigil's remnants. David stood firm, raising his staff—a symbol of his Melchizedekian authority.

As the battle raged, a final surge of faith united the army. Together, they shouted: "If God is for us, who can be against us?" (Romans 8:31).

The battlefield erupted in light, the demons scattering like shadows before the sun. The forces of darkness were defeated, but not eradicated.

Post-Battle Recovery and Strategic Planning

The scene opens in the aftermath of the battle with Lilith, a battle that had tested not only the strength of David and his allies but also their will to stand firm in the face of overwhelming darkness. Their victory, while monumental, came at a high cost. The air was thick with the scent of burnt earth and the acrid smell of spiritual decay left by the forces of evil. The sky above, once vibrant and alive with celestial light, had darkened with an ominous, unholy hue. The sound of faint echoes— like distant cries of fallen warriors—drifted across the mountain range where they had retreated.

Mourning and Healing

As the group gathered at their temporary refuge in a secluded cave near the mountain's peak, an uneasy silence settled over them. David sat cross-legged near the entrance, his brow furrowed in thought. The battle with Lilith had been brutal. His body ached from the physical toll, but it was the mental and spiritual wounds that cut deepest.

One by one, his companions arrived, their faces weary, scarred, and heavy with grief. Some carried bruises, while others bore burns and cuts that had not yet fully healed. The wounds, however, were not merely physical. The spirits of the warriors were wounded, their faith tested by the overwhelming darkness they had just faced.

David's first action was to organize a ceremony of remembrance. They would honor those who had fallen, their sacrifices ensuring the survival of those who remained. But the healing would not stop there. In the farthest corner of the cave, the Seraphim—the highest order of angelic beings—arranged themselves in a circle, their golden eyes glowing with divine radiance. As their wings unfurled, they began to chant, and the sound reverberated throughout the cave like the distant echo of thunder.

One by one, they began to heal the wounded. The divine energy they radiated poured into David and his comrades, soothing their physical wounds. However, it was not without its cost. While the wounds healed, a profound emptiness still lingered within their hearts, a reminder that they had been touched by something far darker than mere mortal battles.

Inner Conflict and Doubt

But even the angels' power couldn't dispel the internal struggles of the group. The feeling of triumph was undercut by nagging doubts. As David watched his comrades, he realized that the victory, though significant, was but one small step in a much greater war.

"Is it over?" one of the warriors, Mara, asked softly. "Is this truly the end of Lilith's influence?"

David's gaze darkened, and his voice was somber when he replied. "No. This is only the beginning."

The words felt heavier than a mountain as he spoke them. Despite their victory, they knew the enemy would regroup, and the fight would continue. They had not destroyed Lilith—only bound her temporarily. Worse still, David feared the unknown consequences of breaking the sigil. Would there be a greater backlash? Had they merely delayed the inevitable?

Mara's question had shaken David deeply, but it was not only her words that left a scar. His mind began to wander, questioning his own worthiness to lead this band of warriors. He thought of his past—the mistakes he had made, the failures, the times he had turned away from the path laid before him. How could someone like him be chosen to lead the army of God against such immense evil?

In the quiet moments, David often found himself alone, wrestling with his insecurities. He doubted whether he was truly the one to fulfill the role of the new Melchizedek. But each time he faltered, a whisper from deep within him reminded him that he was not alone. God had chosen him, and he had to trust in the divine plan—even when the road seemed uncertain.

Strategic Realignment

As they recovered, the group began to regroup, discussing their next move. With Lilith bound, for now, they had a fleeting moment of respite, but David knew they could not afford to waste it. The enemy would be swift to regroup, and they had to be ready.

It was during one of these planning sessions that one of David's closest allies, Elias, proposed a daring plan.

"I say we strike at the heart of their power," Elias said, his voice tinged with urgency. "We go after the core of their operations. We cripple their networks. We don't wait for them to come after us."

David paused, considering Elias' words. It was a bold move, but one that carried immense risk. If they attacked now, would they be throwing themselves into a trap?

"We must act quickly," Elias pressed. "We know the dark forces are gathering their strength. If we strike first, we may have a chance to weaken them before they can retaliate."

But not all were convinced. Several members of the group voiced concerns, suggesting that such a move might be too hasty. Perhaps, they argued, they shouldwait until they had more intelligence about the enemy's next steps. It was a classic divide between the cautious and the bold, and David found himself caught in the middle.

For a moment, he thought back to the ancient manuscripts he had uncovered, filled with prophecies about the coming battle. What did they say about such a decision? Would they be playing into the hands of the enemy by acting too soon? Or was this their only chance to shift the tide in their favor?

The weight of responsibility pressed heavily on him. As the new Melchizedek, David knew that his decisions would shape the future. It was not just his life at stake —it was the fate of all humankind.

David's Leadership Tested

That night, as the group rested, David sat alone, reflecting on everything that had happened. His mind turned to the words of the Psalms—words that had comforted him through the darkest times of his life. One verse in particular echoed through his mind: "The Lord is my shepherd; I shall not want. He maketh me to lie down in green pastures: he leadeth me beside the still waters. He restoreth my soul. He leadeth me in the paths of righteousness for his name's sake." (Psalm 23:1-3)

He realized then that no matter how uncertain the road ahead, he was not walking it alone. With God as his shepherd, he would find the strength to lead.

The next morning, David gathered his allies. The time for doubts was over. They had come this far, and there was no turning back now.

"We strike at dawn," David said firmly, his voice steady and resolute. "We will hit them where it hurts most. And we will not falter."

The group nodded in agreement; their faith renewed. With their wounds healing and their spirits lifted, they were ready for the next phase of their journey.

The Dawn of the Next Step

As the first light of dawn crept over the peaks of the mountain range, the silence was broken by the sound of boots against rocky terrain. David and his allies had made their decision. The enemy was not just a lingering threat—they were a rising force that had to be met with strength, decisiveness, and unwavering faith. The time for hesitation was over.

Their plan was simple: strike at the heart of the enemy's operations. While Lilith was temporarily bound, the dark forces would regroup, and David knew they would soon retaliate. The sigil's breaking had left an opening, and they had to take advantage of it. This would be no small feat, but they had the element of surprise and a band of warriors ready to fight and die for the cause.

Into the Enemy's Heart

As they made their way down the mountainside, the world around them seemed eerily still. It was as if the earth itself was holding its breath, anticipating the coming clash. Each step they took was deliberate, the weight of the task at hand pressing heavily upon them.

David's mind raced as he pondered the risks. They would have to infiltrate the enemy's stronghold, an ancient citadel built into the very heart of the earth. Hidden beneath the mountains, it was a place where the dark forces had gathered to summon demonic armies and orchestrate their plans. The citadel was fortified, its walls imbued with ancient magic that could sense any intrusion.

But David had an advantage—the new power he had unlocked within himself. His connection to the divine had grown stronger, the whispers of ancient knowledge louder. He knew that his destiny was entwined with this battle, and that God had given him the tools necessary to lead. The question was: would it be enough?

Betrayal and Revelation

As the group neared the citadel, David felt the presence of something dark and sinister watching them. It was an unsettling feeling, one that gnawed at him.

Something was wrong. He turned to Elias, his most trusted ally, and saw a flicker of hesitation in his eyes.

"What's wrong?" David asked, his voice low.

Elias paused before speaking, his voice strained. "I don't think we're alone."

At that moment, a figure stepped out from the shadows, a familiar silhouette that sent a chill down David's spine. It was Mara—one of their own. But the look in her eyes was not the same. There was no trace of the warrior he had known. Her gaze was cold, unfeeling.

"You were always meant to fail," Mara's voice was eerily calm, like a whispered prophecy.

David's heart sank. He had suspected that there was a traitor in their midst, but the reality of it hit him like a fist to the gut. Mara had been corrupted by the dark forces, her soul twisted by the very power they sought to destroy.

"You were never meant to lead," Mara continued, her voice thick with venom. "The Melchizedek line is a lie. You are nothing more than a pawn."

The words struck David like a thunderclap, reverberating through him. His doubts had been growing, but hearing them spoken aloud shattered him. Was he really the Melchizedek? Was it all a divine deception?

Before David could react, Mara unleashed a surge of dark energy that crackled through the air, sending sparks flying. The ground trembled beneath them as she called upon the full force of the enemy's power.

But David's resolve, though shaken, remained strong. He drew upon the divine energy within him, calling forth the strength of the Seraphim, binding Mara with a wave of light. She shrieked, her form twisting and contorting as she was momentarily consumed by the radiant force.

The enemy had tried to strike first, but David had held firm. His faith in God, in his purpose, and in the mission ahead, had not faltered.

Two Hundred Twenty-Six

With Mara's betrayal temporarily dealt with, the group pushed forward, reaching the citadel's towering gates. They had no time to waste. The battle was coming, and the dark forces were gathering.

Inside the citadel, the enemy's army was readying for war. Demons —twisted, grotesque creatures with otherworldly strength—stood at attention, awaiting their orders. And at the center of the citadel, a familiar figure waited: Lilith, now freed from her bindings, her form a vision of unearthly beauty and terror.

The confrontation with Lilith was swift, but brutal. She lashed out with dark energy, her power unlike anything they had faced before. But David, strengthened by his connection to the divine and his role as the new Melchizedek, stood tall.

With a word, he summoned the light of the Seraphim, striking Lilith with a blow that momentarily shattered her form. But she was not so easily defeated. Her laugh rang through the citadel, an echo of pure evil.

"You think you can defeat me?" she hissed. "I am the mother of all that is corrupt. You cannot destroy me."

But David stood firm, his warriors behind him. They had fought too long, too hard, to turn back now. The sigil—broken in the depths of the citadel—flared brightly, and a surge of power erupted from within, binding Lilith in chains of light. For now, she was defeated. But David knew it was only temporary.

"We are not done yet," David declared. "This battle is far from over. But we will fight until the end, no matter the cost."

A Divine Message

With Lilith bound once more, the group retreated to their hidden refuge in the mountains. The battle had been won, but the war was far from over.

It was then that God sent a message—a spiritual calling to the sleepers, those who were yet to be awakened. In the stillness of the night, a voice echoed through the mountains, soft but unyielding.

"Awake, O sleepers. Arise from your slumber, for the time has come. The battle for the soul of the earth is at hand. Go into the mountains, where you will be trained. The Davidic priesthood will guide you, and you shall be prepared for the final battle."

David, hearing the voice, knew that this was no mere dream. He had been chosen to lead, not only his companions but an army of the faithful. The prophecy was unfolding before him, and his role—his true identity—was being revealed. He was a direct descendant of Shem, the son of Noah. His bloodline ran back to the ancient times, to the very foundations of the earth.

The knowledge hit him with the weight of a thousand years. He was Melchizedek—priest, king, and leader of God's army.

The Call to Arms

And so, the journey continued. As the armies of darkness regrouped, the time had come for David and his new followers to gather strength. The mountains would become their sanctuary, and in the days to come, they would train and prepare for the final, decisive battle.

The Seraphim had already marked their path. The army of God was growing, ready to take on the enemy in a battle unlike any the earth had ever known.

Would they emerge victorious, or would the darkness claim the world for its own?

The answer lay in the hearts of those who stood with David—the chosen Melchizedek.

As David and his companions made their way deeper into the mountains, they found themselves surrounded by an eerie quiet. The kind of silence that seemed to hum with the weight of an impending storm, as though the very air was thick with anticipation. The retreat was not just a tactical move—it was a sacred space, a place where they could regroup, heal, and prepare for what was coming. God's message to the sleepers echoed in David's mind, growing louder with each step they took toward the hidden valley where they would establish their base.

The mountain sanctuary was more than just a place of safety. It was the foundation of their next move, the training ground for those who had been called to rise up and fight against the dark forces. As they set up camp, a strange sense of unity began to form among them. This was not just a band of warriors, but a new fellowship, a new family—bound together by purpose, faith, and the shared knowledge of the spiritual awakening that was unfolding.

The next days were spent in prayer, meditation, and preparation. David felt a deep stirring in his soul, the ancient bloodline within him waking to the task ahead. It was during these quiet moments that God's calling became clear. He had to train the new converts—not just as soldiers, but as priests. They would be the Davidic priesthood, tasked with guiding the faithful and leading them into the final battle.

THE PRIESTLY CALL

The first new recruits arrived in the mountain valley at dawn, their faces etched with a mix of confusion and awe. These were the sleepers—the ones who had been called from their slumber. Some were young, some old, some experienced warriors, others untested. All of them had felt the pull, the whisper of the divine summoning them to this place. The air seemed to crackle with the power of their arrival, each of them stepping into their destiny.

David stood before them, his heart heavy with the responsibility that had been placed upon him. He knew that he had been chosen for this task, but the weight of it still made him pause.

"You are here for a reason," David said, his voice steady but filled with conviction. "You have been called to something greater than yourselves. You will learn to fight, yes. But more than that, you will learn to serve. You will be priests and warriors, the bearers of the light in a world that is drowning in darkness."

The recruits stood silently, absorbing the words. The task ahead of them was monumental, but they knew they had no choice but to answer the call.

As they began their training, David took the time to teach them the old ways—the ways of Shem, the priesthood of Melchizedek, and the ancient rites that had been passed down through the ages. There was power in these rites, power that would be essential in the coming battle. The new converts were hungry for this knowledge, and the bond between them and their leader grew stronger with each passing day.

DAVID'S REVELATION

It was during one of these intense training sessions, while studying ancient manuscripts in the heart of the mountain's hidden temple, that David uncovered a truth that would change everything. He had always known there was something special about his lineage, but the full weight of it didn't hit him until he poured over an ancient scroll that contained a forgotten prophecy.

The prophecy spoke of a descendant of Shem, a direct heir to the Melchizedek priesthood, who would rise in the last days to lead God's army in the final battle against the forces of evil. The Melchizedek lineage was a rare and sacred one, and David realized, with a mixture of awe and trepidation, that he was the one foretold in the scriptures.

The truth was undeniable: He was the new Melchizedek, chosen to lead God's army in the greatest battle of all time. His bloodline had been kept secret for centuries, hidden in the shadows until the moment it was needed most. And that moment had arrived.

The realization shook him to his core, but it also solidified his resolve. He was not just a leader. He was a high priest, a king, and a warrior. And his destiny was to stand against the forces of darkness with everything he had.

THE BATTLE UNFOLDS

The dark forces were gathering, their legions of demons preparing to invade the earth once more. They were not just content with conquering the mortal realm— they sought to tear down the very fabric of creation itself. They would stop at nothing to bring the world into eternal darkness.

But David and his army were ready. With the power of the Seraphim behind them, the new Davidic priesthood stood at the forefront of the battle. They were not just trained in combat; they were anointed with the divine power of the Most High. The Seraphim, those ancient and mighty beings, were their allies in this war.

They stood beside David, their fiery wings lighting the way, their swords of light cutting through the darkness.

The battle was fierce. The sky itself seemed to rip open as angels and demons clashed, their power shaking the heavens and the earth. The ground trembled beneath their feet as the forces of good and evil collided in a cataclysmic confrontation.

David, now fully realizing his role as Melchizedek, led the charge. His sword—blazing with divine fire—cut through the demonic ranks, and his voice rang out in battle cries that stirred the hearts of his followers.

"Fear not! For God is with us!" he shouted, his voice echoing across the battlefield.

The angels fought with a fury and precision that only the heavenly host could muster. The demons, twisted and corrupt, raged in response, their roars shaking the earth. But despite their might, they could not withstand the onslaught of divine power.

In the midst of the battle, David found himself face to face with the enemy's general—a towering demon with eyes like burning coals. It was Lilith, her form now fully restored and more powerful than ever.

"You think you can defeat me?" she hissed, her voice laced with venom. "You are nothing! You are just a man."

David's heart burned with righteous fury. "I am not just a man," he said, his voice steady and full of divine power. "I am the Melchizedek, Gods chosen warrior, and you will fall before me."

With a mighty blow, he struck down Lilith, sending her crashing to the ground. But even as she fell, she let out a final, bone-chilling laugh. "You have won this battle," she sneered. "But the war is far from over."

The battle raged on, but David knew that this was only the beginning. The forces of darkness would continue to rise, but now he and his army—trained, prepared, and anointed by the divine—were ready for whatever came next.

Victory and the Path Forward

As the dust settled on the battlefield, David stood victorious, his sword raised high. The Seraphim had fought valiantly, their celestial fire having consumed the demonic forces. The army of God had triumphed.

But the war was far from over. The forces of darkness would regroup, they would strike again. And David knew that it would be up to him to lead his followers in the next phase of the battle.

The journey ahead was long, but they had won the first battle, a most crucial victory. And with God's guidance, they would continue to fight.

David's thoughts turned to the prophecy, to his heritage, and to the greater task at hand. The final battle loomed on the horizon, and it would be a battle that would decide the fate of the world.

But for now, there was rest. There was recovery. And there was preparation. Because in the end, the war would not be won by strength alone. It would be won by faith, by righteousness, and by the divine power of God's chosen warriors.

DAVID'S VISION:

As David slept that night; he dreamed. The smoky field engulfed David's senses, the acrid stench of sweat and blood clinging to the back of his throat. His vision swam as pain radiated from his side, a wet warmth pooling against his armor. Disoriented, he clutched at the reins of his steed, feeling its muscles tense beneath him, every breath of the animal labored and steaming in the cold air. Shadows shifted in the smoky haze, then the thunder of hooves shattered the silence.

"Rally to the King! To the King!" The voices rang out, cutting through the chaos.

David turned his head, his breath quickening. Knights clad in polished silver armor charged past him, their shields glinting despite the dim, ash-gray skies. The formation tightened into a V, and before he realized it, he was in the lead, gripping a gleaming majestic sword, with silver filagree around the entire handle.

David's breathing came in gasps, his chest heaving against the weight of the dream. No, it wasn't just a dream. It felt too vivid, too rooted in something ancient, like fragments of a forgotten life or a warning sent across time.

As his surroundings shifted, the battlefield returned. The muddy plains underfoot gave way to the sharp clang of steel on steel. Blood soaked into the earth as the cries of men and horses filled the air. David found himself astride his warhorse again, the beast's muscles taut beneath him, its flared nostrils sucking in air thick with smoke and death.

A banner flapped in the wind, its crest unrecognizable yet oddly familiar—red and gold, a dragon entwined with a crown. David's heart thundered as though it understood a truth his mind could not. He was the King they called to, the figure at the heart of their charge. But why? The question vanished as the horizon erupted with an advancing enemy, dark figures shimmering in the haze like shadows made flesh.

Then, as swiftly as it had begun, the scene fractured. The smoky field became a winding path of white stone. The sound of rushing water filled his ears. David glanced around to find himself walking through an ancient fortress. Its walls were etched with runes glowing faintly, almost imperceptibly, beneath the touch of torchlight. A figure emerged—a bald man in a flowing robe, his staff crowned with a jewel that pulsed faintly as though alive.

David felt words vibrate in the air, though he could not make them out. The man's lips moved with urgent counsel, his expression both fierce and sorrowful.

His pulse quickened as an overwhelming sense of duty and sorrow washed over him. Before he could grasp it, the fortress melted away.

The rushing water faded, replaced by the deafening roar of battle. David stood on a different field among warriors clad in white tunics adorned with crimson crosses, their swords gleaming as they clashed with an enemy cloaked in darkness. The air was thick with the smell of sweat, blood, and damp earth.

David's sword swung through the air, catching the blade of an opponent before plunging into his chest. The man fell with a grunt, his lifeless body hitting the ground. The battlefield churned with chaos, and yet there was an order to it—a shared purpose among the men who fought beside him. A cry broke out nearby: "Protect the Holy Land! Rally to the Cross!"

Through the chaos, David's eyes caught sight of a figure—dark-skinned, bearded man, with piercing eyes as black as obsidian. Their gazes locked, and David felt an unspoken recognition, as though this man had been his enemy for lifetimes. As their swords clashed, the clang of steel echoed like thunder, and David felt a searing pain in his side.

"Saladin!" a voice cried out as the man fell, a look of betrayal and despair etched across his face.

David stumbled backward, clutching his side. He gasped for air, his vision blurring as the battlefield dissolved into smoke and shadow.

The smell of decay hit him next, sharp and acrid, as he opened his eyes. He was no longer on the battlefield but on a desolate shoreline. The waves lapped at the shore, their crimson hue staining the sands. The water was thick, oily, and clogged with the corpses of sea creatures bloated and grotesque. Ash fell from the sky like snow, clinging to his skin and filling his lungs.

David stumbled forward, his boots crunching on the charred remains of wood and bone. In the distance, half-sunken ships jutted from the water like skeletal remains, their masts broken and splintered. The stench of death hung heavy in the air.

"My God," he whispered, his voice breaking. "What is this?"

He fell to his knees, his hands trembling as he dug into the sand, searching for answers in the lifeless landscape. He looked up and saw bodies—human bodies —strewn across the shore. Their faces were frozen in expressions of anguish, their mouths open in silent screams.

David turned away, tears streaming down his face, but his surroundings offered no solace. The skies above were dark, churning with clouds that pulsed with an unnatural red light. A deep rumble shook the ground beneath him, and he turned to see the waves rising higher and higher, as though the sea itself were alive and seeking vengeance.

In the distance, a figure appeared on the horizon, cloaked in shadow. It held a staff that glowed faintly, its light cutting through the darkness. David felt drawn to it, though fear gripped his heart. As he took a step forward, the ground beneath him crumbled, and he fell into a void of swirling smoke and ash.

THE VISION OF TRIBULATION

The void into which David fell gave way to a new scene. He stood amidst a smoldering cityscape. Towers of glass and steel were reduced to jagged ruins, their skeletons silhouetted against a sky that churned with fire and ash. The sun was obscured, casting an eerie twilight over the world. Screams echoed from every direction, but no source could be seen.

David was drawn forward, his feet dragging as though the air itself resisted him. He came upon a massive field, where rows of men and women knelt before a towering idol. The figure was monstrous, crafted of gold and obsidian, with eyes of fire that burned into the souls of those who gazed upon it. The worshipers bore a mark on their foreheads, a sigil unfamiliar yet unnervingly ancient. They chanted in unison, their voices hollow, calling out the name of Belial.

At the base of the idol, David saw the Sons of Belial—shadowed figures cloaked in malevolence. Their presence was suffocating, their laughter a discordant melody of triumph. They moved among the people, whispering lies and granting promises of power, wealth, and immortality to those who pledged fealty. Some resisted, but their cries of defiance were silenced by dark tendrils that emerged from the idol itself, consuming them in flames.

David's heart sank as he saw children among the kneeling masses, their small hands clutching at their parents' robes, their faces etched with fear. He tried to move toward them, to cry out, but his voice was swallowed by the oppressive silence.

The Unleashing of Wrath

The scene shifted again. The earth quaked violently, splitting open to reveal rivers of fire that poured into the city. The seas rose, swallowing entire regions, their waters polluted and blackened. Pestilence swept through the lands, leaving cities desolate and corpses piled high. The skies rained hail and fire, while the winds carried screams that seemed to come from the very bowels of hell.

Above it all, David saw the Sons of Belial orchestrating the chaos. They rallied armies of the damned—humans, demons, and creatures born of nightmares. The armies clashed with a ragged resistance of faithful believers, their banners bearing the symbol of the lamb. Though outnumbered, the faithful fought with unwavering courage, their eyes fixed on the heavens.

In the distance, David saw a figure standing atop a mountain, cloaked in radiant light. Though the figure's face was obscured, David knew it was the King, it was him—the source of hope for the resistance. The figure raised a hand, and the skies began to part, revealing an army of seraphim descending on wings of fire. The battle intensified, and David felt the weight of the conflict pressing down on him, threatening to crush his spirit.

The Awakening and Acts 20:24

David awoke with a start, his body drenched in sweat, his chest heaving as though he'd just run a marathon. The visions lingered in his mind, vivid and horrifying.

He fell to his knees beside his bed, trembling as he tried to make sense of what he had seen.

"Why, Lord?" he whispered. "Why show me this?"

His Bible lay open on the bedside table, and his eyes fell upon the verse he had read the night before: "However, I consider my life worth nothing to me; my only aim is to finish the race and complete the task the Lord Jesus has given me—the task of testifying to the good news of God's grace." (Acts 20:24)

The words anchored him, silencing the storm of fear and doubt that raged within. He understood that the vision was not meant to paralyze, but to fortify him.

SEASON OF SOLITUDE

David sat alone on the cold stone ledge, the wind cutting through him like a thousand whispered accusations. Around him, the mountains stretched into infinity— great shadows rising and falling beneath a gray, unmoving sky. There was no sun, only a pale light diffused through a veil of heavy clouds, as though even heaven mourned with him. His breath misted in the thin air, rising and disappearing like faint prayers unfulfilled.

The weight he carried pressed harder with each passing day, a burden that seemed carved into his very soul. His hands, calloused and trembling, were folded in his lap, his head bowed low. Everything felt so heavy. The silence of the mountains was a vast nothingness, broken only by the wind sweeping across the rocks and valleys. He could not shake the sense that the world itself was holding its breath.

"Why does this feel so heavy?" he cried into the void. His voice, raw and cracking, was carried away on the wind. "Why do I feel so alone? God, do You hear me?

Am I the only one who sees what's coming? Am I the only one left?" Tears fell, hot against his chilled skin, as David sank to his knees. His heart ached in his chest, a hollow cavern carved out by years of loss, sacrifice, and isolation. He thought of Elijah, standing on Mount

Horeb, crying out to God in the very same way, convinced he was utterly alone. I have been very zealous for the Lord God Almighty... I am the only one left, and now they are trying to kill me too. The prophet's words felt like his own.

"Where are You, Lord?" David whispered hoarsely. "Where are Your people? Why does this silence crush me so?"

The silence lingered for a moment longer, but then—a change.

The air stilled, the wind hushed as though commanded into submission. David felt it first on his skin, the hairs on his neck rising as warmth, soft and otherworldly, washed over him. He looked up, and what he saw froze him in place.

A figure stood before him—radiant yet gentle, its very presence soothing the ache in David's chest. The angel's form shimmered, as though woven of pure light, draped in a robe of glowing white. Its face was serene and filled with unspeakable compassion, yet its countenance bore a strength that could shatter mountains.

Wings, vast and luminous, stretched behind the figure, bending the air with their weightless beauty.

David fell back, his hands shielding his eyes from the brightness.

"Fear not," the angel said, its voice like the sound of many waters— powerful yet tender, resonating deep within David's spirit.

David's trembling eased as he lowered his hands, peering up into the angel's face.

"You are not alone," the angel continued, stepping closer. "The Lord has set you apart for this season so that you may hear Him clearly. Even in your solitude, He

is walking with you. Do not mistake silence for abandonment. The weight you bear is heavy because you have been chosen to carry it—but it is not yours to carry alone."

David's chest heaved as the angel's words pierced the dark fog of his mind. "Then why?" he choked out. "Why must I feel this? This emptiness, this isolation?"

The angel knelt beside him, and David could feel the warmth of its presence like a fire in the cold.

"It is in solitude that faith is refined," the angel said softly. "You have been called to lead, and leaders are shaped in the quiet places, in the wilderness where all else is stripped away. It is here you will learn to rely fully on Him, for there is no other."

David blinked, tears streaming unchecked down his face.

"But..." he whispered, "what if I can't do this? What if I fail?"

"You will not fail," the angel replied, "for the strength you seek does not come from within yourself, but from the Almighty. You are not alone, David. There are seven thousand who walk in quiet faith, unseen but waiting. They are as you are—sleeping in discernment, their hearts prepared by the Lord for the day they are

called. At the appointed time, they will rise. God's army is not small, and you are not its only soldier."

David's breath caught. Seven thousand. Seven thousand others. The words struck a chord deep within him, a glimmer of hope blooming in the dark recesses of his mind.

"Seven thousand," he repeated, as though testing the words.

The angel smiled, a light of joy flickering in its divine gaze. "Seven thousand. And you will not walk alone. God is always with you, David, even in this season of solitude. His Spirit will strengthen you, as it did for Elijah. His angels will minister to you, as they did for Jesus. You are not forgotten."

David's shoulders sagged as the weight he carried seemed, for the first time in weeks, to ease. The angel stood, and with it rose a soft glow, surrounding them both.

"Rise, David," the angel commanded gently. "Be strong and courageous. For the days to come will demand all of you—but the Lord will supply all you need."

David's body felt renewed strength as he rose to his feet, the angel's presence still humming in the air. He wiped his face, his tears replaced by determination. He was not alone. He had been set apart for a purpose. And though the road ahead would be fraught with darkness, he knew he would not walk it in vain.

The silence returned as the angel vanished, the mountains as still as they had been before. But now, David saw them differently. They were no longer oppressive —they were a refuge. A place where God spoke in whispers to those willing to listen.

Lifting his eyes to the gray skies, David whispered: "I consider my life worth nothing to me; my only aim is to finish the race and complete the task the Lord Jesus has given me—the task of testifying to the good news of God's grace."

And to vanquish Gods enemies.

The words hung in the air...